Eclectic Witchery

Ailie Hunter
and
Garry Jeffrey-Nixon

GREEN MAGIC

Green Magic
53 Brooks Road
Street
Somerset BA16 0PP
England

www.greenmagicpublishing.com

Designed & typeset by K.DESIGN
Winscombe, Somerset

ISBN 9781916014084

GREEN MAGIC

CONTENTS

CHAPTER ONE

IT'S RITUAL TIME

Magick is old. In ancient times the world seemed more mysterious and dangerous, and magick gave people the power and confidence to navigate the unknown around them. Supernatural forces were thought to govern everything: weather, plagues, fortune, disaster, crops, love, children – you name it. Amulets and incantations were used to protect against storms and dark forces. Gods were invoked, worshipped, and appeased daily in some cases. A class of priests and priestesses and other disciples came forth to serve the early deities. The world's earliest known poet was Enheduanna (2285–2250 BCE), who was High Priestess of the Goddess Inanna.

In modern Western Paganism, there's such a vast variety of beliefs that we wouldn't attempt to cover them all in this book. Nonetheless, common practices and beliefs among British Pagans include revering nature, believing in the transformational power of magick, life after death, the spirit realm, and gods and goddesses. Appreciation of the seasons also links modern Pagans to our ancestors, who looked on life and nature as both magical and divine.

The sun blesses the planet with light and warmth, and the moon looks over the Earth while it sleeps. Winter is a time of death, rest and hibernation for animals who store fat to see them through winter. The bare starkness of the trees' skeletal fingers reach towards the sun in the faith its strength will return to rejuvenate them. Spring is a time of rebirth, hope and regeneration, and looking forward. Summer is a time of abundance and life, when the trees are in full leaf and the flowers are blooming and feeding the insects, and young animals run through the land. Autumn gives a variety of colour in nature and a wide range of foods are harvested then too. Honouring these seasons, the Earth and her creatures, and both male and female aspects of divinity, are common Pagan values.

THE SUN AND THE MOON

In the morning the sun rises in the east, bringing light and creating the day. It's a good time to pray or give thanks for the day ahead, connect with divinity and ask for the kind of day you want – to achieve a goal or for blessings for friends, family or the Earth.

The sun disappears daily into the west and the north – the magical quarter. The north is symbolic of the Earth, of quiet, peace, and mountains, and it's a favourite direction for witches to face when practicing magick, although east is also used a lot, as is the north east.

In the old world, the Greeks had Apollo, the Egyptians Ra. The sun disk that the Pharaohs wore was the symbol of Ra, and myth had it that the scarab beetle God Kheper rolled the sun disk across the heavens through the day.

Modern Pagans use the Sun God during the celebrations of the wheel of the year, as the sun progresses upwards through the sky for the six months when it is waxing – taking in the four festivals of light – then lowers during the rest of the year – taking in the four dark festivals, going through a cycle of life and death and rebirth.

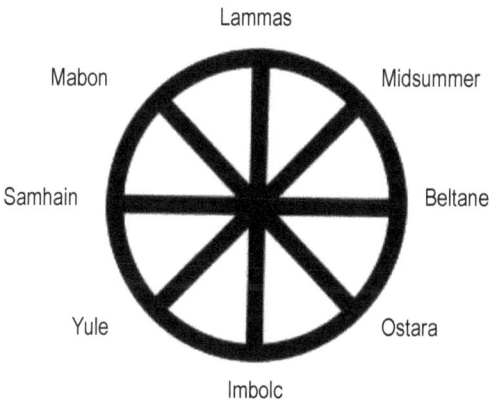

Lammas

Mabon — Midsummer

Samhain — Beltane

Yule — Ostara

Imbolc

The moon is the Goddess. She affects the tides of the sea and the inner moods and emotions of people. The moon also rises in the east, and travels across the sky, although you sometimes see the moon in the north in the mornings. In Paganism, the moon is worshipped as a Triple Goddess – Maiden, Mother and Crone or waxing, full and waning moons.

The Maiden aspect of the moon represents youth and childhood, freedom, and increasing light. It's a good time to give and send positivity. The Maiden aspect is growing in strength every day until the moon is full, and on a personal level it is a good time to bring things into your own life. She rules hope, inspiration, new beginnings and adventures.

The full moon Goddess is the Mother, where the Goddess reaches the pinnacle of womanhood and is at her best. It's good to be giving at this point and put the interests of your children and others before yourself. The full moon is also great for healing and for most magic.

The Crone Goddess or waning moon represents wisdom, lessons learned and experience of life that can be passed on. As the moon wanes, do magick to get rid of negativity and push away undesirable circumstances. Look to the future, and seek answers during the wise Crone's time.

The Sun God and Moon Goddess represent the male and female. The Moon Goddess is connected to dreaming, the dark sky, psychism, mystery, illusion, imagination, emotion, mood, the unconscious mind and the menstrual cycle. There are many Moon Goddesses, and some Sun Goddesses.

WHAT IS RITUAL?

Rituals differ depending on the time of year, and the reason for it. A ritual can be to give thanks, to honour the gods for what we receive, and to ask for things which could help us in life.

In springtime, or around Imbolc, give thanks for the light and for the dark days passing. Around harvest times such as Lammas or Mabon you can give thanks for abundance. Lammas is the bread harvest and Mabon is the fruit harvest.

In the past Samhain was a time to slaughter the cattle that wouldn't make it through winter, and salt the meat, and keep the strongest of the herd. Nowadays, everything we do is symbolic; we put food, mead or wine onto the ground as a gift to the gods.

Rituals can be simple, like sitting in a sunny field or under moonlight, but a common ritual shape is:

THE BASIC RITUAL SHAPE

Cleanse space with a broom and/or incense/saltwater.

Cast a circle.

Call quarters.

Call God/Goddess and bid hail and welcome, and/or do magical work.

Give thanks/cakes and wine/bid hail and farewell.

Release quarters.

Release circle.

A CLEANSING BATH

A cleansing bath before ritual rids you of any impurities you may have picked up during the day. To have a cleansing bath, light candles and have incense burning if you like it. Try and make it a magical bath, meditative, maybe think about your intent for the ritual, add essential oils, salts or scents, and relax. If you don't have time for one though, you could anoint yourself instead with oil.

CLEANSING THE SPACE

It is common to cleanse the area in which you will be working by either symbolically sweeping the area with a broom or by cleansing the area with incense, saltwater or sage.

GROUNDING

Grounding is a good way to dissipate any energy which has attached itself to you. It also brings you back to earth after a ritual. It helps you go from a heightened sense back to level-headed reality. It's good to ground both at the start and end of magical work. Different ways to ground are: stamping feet and shaking hands, touching the roots or base of a tree, touching the earth with bare feet or the palms of your hands (both), putting your back to a tree and letting the tree take the energy from you, or running hands under cold water.

There's increasing evidence that grounding is good for your health. It balances the electrical charge in your body and regulates some unconscious processes which promote wellbeing and sleep. I've also, in the past, found grounding works as a painkiller, I would put my hands on the earth or in water and ask the Goddess to remove the pain and take that energy to a place where it could do good.

ALTARS: CREATING AND BLESSING

An altar usually sits dormant when not in use, with a pentagram, a statue or other ornaments. When working, place saltwater for blessing, favourite crystals, candles for the God and Goddess, ritual tools such as an athame, a wand, or statues and items which represent what you want to do. To bless an altar, use the elements. You can devote an altar to the God and Goddess in general or to a particular God or Goddess.

To Bless an Altar

> Light incense and candles first, have saltwater ready, and flowers.
>
> Cast a circle and call the quarters.
>
> Call the God and Goddess to witness the blessing (in your own words or something like the below).
>
> *I call the Goddess to witness this blessing of my altar and tools in Her name.* (Optional candle) *Hail and Welcome.*
>
> *I call the God to witness this blessing of my altar and tools in His name.* (Optional candle) *Hail and Welcome.*
>
> Pass the incense over the altar and pass the tools through it, bless the flowers as well (put these outside as an offering after the ritual).

Sprinkle the altar and tools with saltwater.

I bless this altar and these tools in the name of the God and Goddess and the elements Fire, Air, Earth and Water, and dedicate it to magical work. So mote it be.

Dear God and Goddess, thank you for your presence during this consecration, leave if you must, stay if you will.

Release the quarters and circle.

Making Saltwater

There are a few ways to do this, such as this simple blessing:

Take spring water, and sea-salt, and bless:

I bless this salt in the name of the God and the Goddess, to remove negativity and make it fit for purpose.

Then mix the salt into the water and bless:

I bless this water in the name of the God and the Goddess, to remove negativity and make it fit for purpose.

If you are blessing water at the full moon and you can see it, hold the water up to the moon and visualise the Goddess blessing it and the surface of the water shining silver.

CASTING CIRCLES

You cast a circle to create sacred space, to contain energy, and have a space you can work confidently and safely within. It isn't always needed, but in a group, it is usually good to cast one.

Casting a Circle (example)

> Start in the north – people always thought magick came from the north. It is connected to the rising of the sun which dies in the west and is reborn in the east. So, the north is in between dark and light. Use your hand, a wand, an athame or your imagination. You are casting a sphere, and can imagine a purple light encircling you. Start to speak when you come to the east.

> *I cast this circle in the name of the God and Goddess to protect us while we work our rite this night/day.*

Some people call quarters before the circle, some afterwards. Some people verbally release circles, some do it widdershins (anticlockwise), and some do it deosil (clockwise).

> *I release this circle with thanks. The circle is open but unbroken. May the love of the Goddess be always in our hearts.*

THE DIRECTIONS

East: The Realm of Air. It symbolises rebirth and renewal, dawn, the new day waxing, and new beginnings. The Maiden aspect.

South: The Realm of Fire. It symbolises warmth, heat, dynamic energy, strength, completion, the day itself, the Mother and the Father.

West: The Realm of Water. Fluidity, cleansing, raw energy. The moon begins to take over at this point. Waning time, leading to darkness.

North: The Realm of Earth. The magical point. The darkest and most quiet point. Peace and tranquillity. Night-time.

Centre: The Realm of Spirit. Here lies divinity and the spirit realm, the unchanging nature, the eternal energy behind all life. The ancestors. All time and space.

CALLING QUARTERS, EXAMPLES OF QUARTERS

The quarters are called at the points of the directions, to guard the circle and to add to the magical intent of a rite. Calling the quarters helps you concentrate on the energies of the points, and manifest the qualities of that particular direction. The Watchtowers are commonly called, but other options are power animals or archangels.

Power Animals

To invoke:

(Face East) *I call upon the powers of Air, soaring eagle, glide through the skies, and come to us to guard the gateway of the east. Hail and Welcome.*

(Face South) *I call upon the powers of Fire, Phoenix rise from your embers, and come to us to guard the gateway of the south. Hail and Welcome.*

(Face West) *I call upon the powers of Water, returning salmon, come to guard the gateway of the west. Hail and Welcome.*

(Face North) *I call upon the powers of Earth, majestic stag, come to us to guard the gateway of the north. Hail and Welcome.*

To release, you can go round either widdershins from the north or deosil from the east, thanking them and saying Hail and Farewell.

Archangels

To invoke:

(Face East) *Greetings O Raphael, Prince of Air, please enter this circle and bless this magick (guard this rite).*

(Face South) *Greetings O Michael, Prince of Fire, please enter this circle and bless this magick (guard this rite).*

(Face West) *Greetings O Gabriel, Prince of Water, please enter this circle and bless this magick (guard this rite).*

(Face North) *Greetings O Auriel, Prince of Earth, please enter this circle and bless this magick (guard this rite).*

To release:

(Face East) *Hail Raphael, my thanks for your presence and blessings. Hail and Farewell.*

(Face South) *Hail Michael, my thanks for your presence and blessings. Hail and Farewell.*

(Face West) *Hail Gabriel, my thanks for your presence and blessings. Hail and Farewell.*

(Face North) *Hail Auriel, my thanks for your presence and blessings. Hail and Farewell.*

WICCAN QUARTERS

Pentagrams have been used for centuries for protection, and at the cardinal points of a magical circle.

To invoke (starting at east): *Oh Mighty ones of the East/South/West/North, I do summon, stir and call ye up to witness our rites and guard the circle. We bid thee Hail and Welcome.*

At each point, the invoking pentagram for that point is drawn in the air and then charged by touching the centre.

The Banishing and Invoking Elemental Pentagrams

To banish (starting at East and moving deosil): *Oh Mighty powers of the East/South/West/North, I do thank you for your attendance and 'ere you depart to your fair and lovely realms. We bid you Hail and Farewell.*

Use the elemental banishing pentagrams for releasing them.

CAKES AND WINE

Inside the circle but after the ritual, cakes and wine are taken to give energy and as an offering to the gods. In a coven it is usually the High Priest and High Priestess that do this, but anyone can, including a solitary. Below is a Wiccan example.

The High Priest kneels and presents the chalice with wine/mead, the High Priestess is holding the athame, and puts the tip of it into the chalice and draws an invoking Earth pentacle in the fluid and says the charge:

As the athame is to the male, so the cup is to the female, and conjoined they become one in truth, and bring blessedness.

Then the plate of cakes is presented by someone in the circle to the High Priest who would hold it. The High Priestess draws an invoking Earth pentacle with the tip of the athame over them and says:

Oh Queen most secret, bless this food into our bodies, bestowing health, wealth, strength, joy and peace. And the fulfilment of love that is perfect happiness.

MAIDEN, MOTHER, CRONE

Rituals to the Maiden are good for personal growth, youth, vitality, adventure, new times, hope, bringing good things towards you, inspiration and looking forward to the future. Things associated with the Maiden include virginity, innocence, playfulness, white flowers, growing strength and personal power, independence, forests, young animals, and the new and waxing moon.

Example Ritual to the Maiden – In this case Brigid

Cast circle and call quarters.

Light a white candle and call Brigid (horseshoes are lucky to Brigid, as are bells, so you might want to include them on your altar).

Brigid of the new light, we call and welcome you to join us in our rite. Child of the flowers, lady of the spring. May you bring energy and focus to the future. Hail and welcome!

Spend some time connecting to the Goddess. Brigid is a very interesting Goddess who never disappeared from the British Isles due to being made into a saint by Christians and worshipped in that way.

Ask for Brigid's guidance or do whatever work you wanted to do with Her (healing, home blessings, inspiration, and arts and crafts or personal projects are special to Brigid but she can be called for almost anything).

Give an offering to the Goddess – perhaps some flowers on the altar, or honey is good.

Thank Her, and bid Her stay if She will, go if She must.

Release quarters and circle.

Leave offering outside.

Example Ritual to the Mother Goddess – Isis

Rituals to the Mother are good for comfort, love, abundance, birth, good health, maternal messages (for someone who has lost their mother). Associations are pregnancy, motherhood, red flowers, beauty, good fortune, prosperity, teaching the younger generation, the sea, the full moon. In this case, calling on Isis (Aset), a supreme and long-worshipped Goddess who began in Ancient Egypt, and went on to be worshipped in Greece and around the known world at that time, including Britain and Spain. There was a statue to Isis in Notre Dame until the 16th century, and she is depicted inside the Sistine Chapel with Moses. She is a favourite deity of modern Pagans, and is very giving and protective.

Cast circle and call quarters.

Call Isis by chanting Her name or reading aloud about Her from a book, then you could say something like this:

Dearest Mother Isis, Goddess of the Nile, of Magick and of Life and Rebirth, please honour us by joining us in this circle tonight. Hail and welcome, Blessed be!

Spend some time connecting to the Goddess, and do the work you intend with Her (Isis can be called for many purposes but would be good for creative magick, for health and healing, for comfort in loss, and for protection. She is a very powerful Goddess).

Give an offering to mother goddesses such as fruit and grain.

Thank Her, and bid Her stay if She will, go if She must.

Release quarters and circle.

Leave offering outside.

Example Ritual to the Crone – Here the Cailleach

Rituals to the Crone are good for gaining knowledge, for banishing, for moving things away from you, for releasing things and recovering from past mistakes, for endings to make way for new beginnings. Associations with the Crone are black, purple, magical wisdom, the waning moon, the dark moon, death, things which are hidden – such as the occult, and the ancestors.

Cast circle and call quarters.

Call the Goddess.

Mighty Cailleach, Goddess of the Darkness, Goddess of Wisdom, through your portal may you lead us to the light.

Please join us in this celebration and protect us in our rite.

Spend some time connecting to the goddess, and ask for the guidance and understanding you need.

Give an offering to the Cailleach, such as red wine, seasonal berries and mistletoe.

Thank Her, and bid Her stay if She will, go if She must.

Release quarters and circle.

Example Rituals to Gods – Calling the God

Rituals to the God are good for productivity, sport, success, protection, virility, help solving problems, strength, forging ahead, or as a consort to the goddess. Associations are the wilderness, totem animals like stags and bears, the green woodland, and the sun.

Circle and quarters.

Call a god, such as Pan to bring fun, joy and laughter (Pan is also a Green Man God).

Oh Potent Pan, of field and forest,

shepherd of the hills and valleys,

watcher over sheep and goats,

play your syrinx to bring the music of nature to our circle.

Hail to the Muses, who surround you, in the mighty groves,

please join with us now and bless our rite.

OR:

Herne of the Hunt – another Green Man God – who is good for handfasting (since he is a God of fertility). Herne is also good for protection, and to help with problems and injustice.

Herne bring your strength, oh stag of the seven tines.

Let your majesty invoke all that is good and green.

From the earth, to add strength to our ritual,

We bid you hail and welcome.

Work with your intention with the God you've chosen.

Thank him and make an offering – such as mead or wine or beer and mistletoe (the white symbolises the seed and the green symbolises the female) or evergreen foliage.

Invite him to stay or to leave as he pleases, or bid him farewell with thanks.

Release quarters and circle.

RITUAL AS AN ENACTMENT OF MYTH

It's common in group rituals, like the old Mummers, to enact scenarios relating to different pantheons within the circle, such as enacting the Greek myth where Persephone is taken to the underworld, or the battle between the Oak and Holly Kings. At Midsummer, the Oak King (light half of the year) loses to the Holly King (dark half of the year).

Example Enactment Ritual – Lammas and John Barleycorn

Cast circle and call quarters.

Call the God (example Pan) and Goddess (example Demeter).

Almighty Demeter, Goddess of the Harvest, we call upon you to witness our rites and be with us and protect us in our circle. Hail and welcome.

Oh great Pan, God of the Flocks and Mountainsides, we call upon you to witness our rites and be with us and protect us in our circle. Hail and welcome.

At Lammas, the corn is ripe and due to be harvested, John Barleycorn represents the corn being cut. In the ritual someone represents this and holds the corn above his head, and he would be symbolically sacrificed by the one acting as the high priestess. The corn would then fall onto the ground, which also serves as the offering to the God and Goddess (as do the cakes and wine after the ritual).

Think about things you might want to sacrifice or give up from your life (bad habits for example).

Cakes and wine.

Thank the God and Goddess, bid farewell.

Release the quarters and circle.

Put the rest of the cakes and wine on the ground as offerings.

CHAPTER TWO

EVERY LITTLE THING SHE DOES IS MAGICK

Magick and spells work by sending focused intent to the Universe (I use the word magic and magick to mean the same thing throughout the book). During the waxing moon, you can send spells of hope and prayer towards someone who is in need of it, perhaps using candle or knot magic. It's good and easy to write your own spells. Some people like to add a caveat such as 'with harm to none, it is done' rather than just 'so mote it be' at the end, to prevent any magical backfires. There are many spell books out there that people can buy and adapt to their needs. When I began my journey, I devoured lots of books which helped me develop and appreciate the Craft. In my experience, you don't need many ingredients but some people enjoy using a variety of herbs or techniques in spells. There are no guarantees, but it's quite effective if your spells rhyme.

When it comes to using divination before doing a spell, some people do and some don't. If I use the tarot before doing a spell to check the outcome in advance, I would turn three cards. Generally, I look to avoid the 'bad' cards such as the tower, devil, 10 of swords, 3 of swords, 5 of swords and the 9 of swords. I also look at the meanings to see if there's something that doesn't seem compatible with the intended outcome of the magick. Other people might use a pendulum. There's more detail on tarot in Chapter Nine.

Example Knot Spell

To give strength to someone who needs it for any reason – such as to give birth, go to a job interview, or carry something to fruition or get through something. Take a piece of cord (white or a colour related to the goal), hold it out and think of your intent as you tie a loose granny knot and visualise the intent, state the intent aloud, then pull firmly and say 'so mote it be'.

VISUALISING

Visualising for spells is important. If you're doing magic for a person, see their face in your mind. If you are sending blessings for someone in a crisis, see them as completely better. For personal goals, see yourself having already achieved the goal. Fill the images with colour, sound, and anything to make the images stronger. It's like an imaginary painting. Hold the visualisation for 30 seconds, if your mind won't wander. This is the magick of the mind.

CANDLES

Candles are very easy to use for magic. The colour is the key, and the strength of the intent. For love, use a pink or red candle, for healing a white or pale blue candle, green or red are good for power and strength, silver for Goddess work, purple for magical intent such as sending inspiration to someone or to connect with spirit, black for removing negativity or negative people from your life, yellow or orange for success. Again, people have their own associations. Green is also good for prosperity, and is commonly used for the Goddess.

Example Candle Spell to Attract Love

Take a pink or red candle, surround with rose petals or place a rose quartz beside it, anoint the candle with blessed oil from tip to base while visualising your intent strongly. There is no attempt to ensnare someone because that's not a positive intent and would likely backfire. State the intent aloud and what the favourable outcome would be. Then light the candle and add a caveat, 'with harm to none, it is done.' Let it burn out if possible. If not, snuff it out.

Example Candle Spell: From Darkness to Light

A black candle could symbolise someone's depression or another malady that's affecting them. Take the black candle, hold it in the middle and anoint from the centre to the ends without rubbing. Hold it and state your intent – to get rid of the negativity or whatever is affecting the person, light the candle, add a 'with harm to none, it is done.' Let it burn it out, taking away the negative ailment or situation.

BINDING SPELLS

When you bind someone, you are generally doing something against their will, so it's a bit of a no-no, but it depends on the situation and lots of people do it. Binding spells can have long-term effects, and can rebound. A friend of ours did a binding spell on her cheating husband (she doesn't mind us using this story). She made a poppet binding him back to her, to realise his mistake and come home. This has sometimes proved a regret over the years! She would like to go find the poppet and cleanse it, but it is hidden behind a boiler in an old house she has no access to.

Example Binding Spell (The Freezer Spell)

Get a jar to act as an oubliette to hold the person, take a photo or bit of hair or personal item from that person, place it in the jar, state the intent, then bury it or put it in the freezer.

An Alternative: Petition Spell Against Harassment

With a black or blue pen, write the person's name and why you are doing the magic about them, and write that you mean them no harm, that you just want them to stop and move on (this is a good spell for ex-partners who are being a nuisance), and then just burn it.

For stubborn or dangerous situations, I would call on a God or Goddess to remove the person or for protection. Good gods for protection include Herne, Bast, Isis, Hecate, the Morrigan, and the Archangel Michael.

RAISING ENERGY FOR MAGIC

Often spells are done without doing anything additional to raise energy but you can by clapping, dancing or making a noise with rattles, bells, drums or chanting.

To Bring Happiness to Someone

Cast a circle and state intent to bring happiness to that person, then raise energy using drums or dancing or clapping or chanting or anything that makes a noise. Then when you open the circle the energy goes to the person.

NATURE SPELLS

The great outdoors is a great place to do magic, whether in forest clearings, at the beach or in the mountains.

River Spell

Paint or scratch a rune for whatever you need (courage, strength, protection, love, health, luck, etc) onto a stone, hold it to your heart to charge it, and cast it into a river with a statement of intent and thanks.

Autumn Spell

Take a conker or an acorn and push it into the earth, or plant it in a pot, while making a wish. It will grow the next year.

Planting Flowers in the Garden for a Magical Space

Planting seeds, bulbs and flowers adds colour, life, magic and joy to a place. You can do it mindfully to encourage biodiversity by planting native flowers which will attract insects and birds, and add a moon garden if you like (white flowers, night-scented blooms). This will bless the garden with positive energy and fragrance. You could plant at the cardinal points – so yellow flowers in the east, red/orange and pink for the south, purple and blue for the west, and white and green shrubs in the north, and use the space as a magic circle for spell-work. Or light incense out there and candles in jars, and sit out and meditate. Crystals such as rose quartz placed at the cardinal points give a garden additional harmony.

Sun, Sea, Sand Rejuvenation Spell

Go for a sunny walk on a sandy beach (or sit in a quiet spot there if you prefer). Contemplate your life and what you have achieved. Watch the water as it breathes in and out. Think about everything that is going well in your world. Go down to the water and touch it. Imagine for a while that any woes you have are taken away from you as the tides move away. The water cleanses your spirit and body. After a while, remove your hands from the water and raise them to the Sun, imagine the energy of the Sun blessing your being, filling you with its vitality and good health. If you wanted to leave an offering to the place you could offer a seashell, filled with a little earth and sprinkled with seeds, or just leave some food for the local wildlife.

Guidance from the Sun, Moon or Earth

Look in the direction of the Sun, or at the Moon, or sit on the grass with your palms flat on the ground. Ask a question and wait silently until you receive an answer.

Mountain Magic for Transformation

To change from feeling mundane to feeling blessed, go for a hill-walk if you are able, and climb to the top. It is best done in a mindful manner – listening to the sounds and appreciating the views. This is great for a sense of achievement and lifts the soul. The journey to the top will help you clarify things in your life, as the natural world brings enlightenment, absorbs and transforms negativity, and helps get rid of stagnant ways of thinking about an issue. Once at the top, sit and enjoy the view and make a resolution about a change you want to make in your life.

Moon Magick to Bring Magic into your Life

Start with the new moon, and nightly after that towards the full moon, go out each night in any weather and stand under the moon (even if it is hidden behind cloud) and send out to the Goddess your desire for more magic to come into your life, whether you have specific ideas about what you would like to happen, or just as a general wish. As the moon comes to fruition at the full moon, your wish should be granted.

MEDITATION

Meditation changes the state of your mind and body, and puts you into a more spiritual space, where you can access your inner self and gain answers from divinity.

EVERY LITTLE THING SHE DOES IS MAGICK

Example Meditation to the Maiden

Sit in a quiet place, ground, if you like add incense (white sage or lavender or any you like) and/or a candle to change the atmosphere of the moment. Close your eyes and go on a journey to meet the Maiden. See yourself in a forest glade, smell the air, look around, feel the texture of the grass beneath, explore if you want to, wait for the Maiden to come to you, introduce yourself and give an offering of white flowers to Her. Listen to anything She may tell you. If it feels right, ask for advice on something or for inspiration or help with another goal. Spend as much time as you want, then say thanks and goodbye, and gently come back to the present.

Example Meditation to the Mother

Sit in a quiet place, ground, if you like add incense (sandalwood or musk or mugwort are good for the Mother but any you like) and/or a candle to charge the atmosphere. Close your eyes and go on a journey to meet the Mother. See yourself at the sea. Feel the waves breaking over your ankles, your feet in the sand, hear the gulls overhead, smell the saltwater. Walk along the beach if you want, feel the Sun beating down on you, listen to the water lapping, see your footprints in the sand. Wait for the Mother to come to you. Introduce yourself and give Her an offering of wheat or corn. Listen to anything She says. Take comfort from Her, ask for Her advice or help. After a while, say thanks and goodbye, and gently come back to the present.

Example Meditation to the Crone

Sit in a quiet place, ground, if you like add incense (dragon's blood, frankincense or cinnamon are good but any you like the smell of) and/or light a candle. Close your eyes and go on a journey to meet the Crone. See yourself at the edge of a cave, walk inside, wait until you are in darkness and sit down. Wait for the Crone. Introduce yourself and give her an offering of an apple or a raven feather. Listen to anything she says, or ask if there's any wisdom she may want to impart. Ask for the outcome of future events if you like. After a while, say thanks and goodbye, and gently come back to the present.

FOREST BATHING

Forest bathing is a good way of getting rid of stresses and strains from your body or your life and afterwards you should feel cleansed.

Ideally, find a mixed woodland, with different varieties of trees. Choose a particular tree that you are drawn to. Find a quiet spot and sit down with your back to the tree, place your hands onto the ground. Your head should lay against the tree, if you can be barefoot even better. Feel the energy come through the ground and up through the tree, lift your arms up and feel the energy radiating through your fingertips. Then stand up and touch the tree with your hands, lay your forehead against the tree with your third eye touching it, and use your voice to vibrate energy into the tree making a sound, do this for a few minutes, connecting with the tree and the sounds and smells of the environment around you. Once finished, lay your hands on the earth and ground yourself.

CHAPTER THREE

PUTTING THE HERBS IN HERBOLOGY

Through his background as a chef, Garry became interested in herbs – initially for cooking, but he then went on to study herbs for medicines and magical purposes.

Feverfew – medicinal. Painkiller, you can grow it. Good for period pain, muscle pain, headaches. Chew the leaves or make a tincture from them (dried out leaves left in vodka for a couple of months). Contains acetylsalicylic acid.

Dandelion – herbal tea, good for rheumatism and is an antioxidant, you use the roots – they can be picked or bought. Dry them out and make a tea with them, or add butter to the tea to make a creamy latte-like drink.

Mugwort – a very common plant found in coastal areas, can be smoked or put in tea, or made into tinctures to relax you. It can also be burned as an incense in ritual

Valerian – otherwise known as herbal Valium. A sleeping

aid and a sedative, and rescue remedy for panic attacks. You can make your own or buy it in capsule form. You need the root, which is harvested after flowering. Peel and chop up the root, dry it out completely, then once dry add either vodka or gin and leave for two months in a dark place, then filter out the root and compost and use the liquid in a dropper bottle and take six drops on your tongue (don't use when driving).

Elder – elderberries can make good wine and salad dressing, and it is good for the digestive system and has plenty vitamin C. You boil the berries down with sugar, strain out the seeds and flesh, add red wine vinegar, and more brown sugar, bottle it up and refrigerate and it's good for months.

Hawthorn – hawthorn is also a very magical plant. Grow it round your house for protection. The hawthorn tree can make nice wands for dark Goddess magic or banishing spells, and you can also use hawthorn leaves in a beetroot salad.

Rowan – people used to plant them around their homes for protection, and it's a great source of vitamin C. You can make a preserve with crab-apple and sugar or honey (rowan berries are bitter).

Willow – associated with the moon and water, the bark is a good painkiller – the bark contains acetylsalicylic acid which is the same as aspirin. Great for toothache – rub the inside of the bark on your gum for it to go numb, or make a tea by mashing the bark, add boiling water, leave it 5 mins and strain. Or add to a cream to rub on an area.

Meadowsweet – makes fragrant incense. Collect the flowers, dry them, mix with something else like finely dusted cedar bark and burn it. Also, a top painkiller (the roots) – they taste like Germolene.

Sorrel – tastes like apples, very good for digestion, great in salad and has tonnes of vitamins including vitamin D. Make soup with it – adding garlic and veggies.

Mint – good for the stomach and indigestion.

Lemonbalm – a poultice for boils or for bruises – mash up the leaves mix with Vaseline or other cream and put on the area.

Comfrey – edible leaves, fry them up if you bruise easily and eat them or mash them up and rub into affected area. The roots are good as well.

CHAPTER FOUR

THERE'S SOMETHING IN THE AIR: THE ELEMENTS

AIR MAGIC

Working with air is good for bringing lightness to spirit or body, for sending energy to others, for journeys, and all intellectual pursuits.

You can use feathers and incense, work outdoors under the sky or in strong winds, use fans, call the archangel Raphael, call fairies, call bird elementals such as eagles.

Example Air Spell – Sending Energy to Someone in Difficulty

Cast circle.

Call the quarters but concentrate on the east.
Use power animals such as raven for the east,
phoenix for the south, selkie for the west, wolf for

the north. Light candles at each quarter in their honour.

State the purpose of the magic.

Thank and release the three quarters of the south, west and north for their energy and put out their candles (but not the one in the east).

Light a central candle to gather the energies of the other candles. Stand at the east and send the energies raised with a wand or athame to the person you want to help, thank and release eastern quarter.

Release the circle, and let the central candle burn down completely.

MAKING INCENSE

Use some ground cedarwood as a base or other fragrant wood (applewood, hazelwood, hickory, cade, or pinecones ground up with a mortar and pestle). These can be bought in tins or packets online. You can mix in essential oils or other fragrant herbs like rosemary and sage, and add resins like frankincense and dragon's blood. Then burn it with charcoal in a pot (or sometimes the charcoal isn't needed).

If you want to make joss sticks: add more essential oil to the above mixture and take a wooden stick, skewer or thin twig from a tree (let it dry first), and roll it around the mixture and let dry for a few days. Then light as normal incense sticks.

Good incense for Midsummer: mix lime zest, orange zest and lemon zest – not the pith just zest, and put onto a charcoal disk.

For Samhain: dragon's blood, rosemary and sage.

For consecrating magical tools: frankincense, clary sage and rosemary.

FIRE MAGIC

Fire spells are great for passion, energy, health, courage, protection (Archangel Michael). You can use candle magic, or a version of the above air spell leaving the south to last, you can also burn petitions (this can also be air). Dragon's blood incense.

Example Fire Magic for Fertility

You need a fire: cauldron, pit or small bonfire (or candle).

Circle.

Invoke all the quarters with candles, paying attention to the south.

Address the south particularly, stating your intention, and asking for the passion to build up inside you before you jump the fire.

People wanting children would jump over the fire, and anyone around could chant something like this (adapted from *The Wickerman*):

Take the flame inside you, burning down below, fire seed fire seed make the baby grow, take the flame inside you, burning very long, fire seed fire seed make the baby strong. Take the flame inside you, burning very high, fire seed fire seed, make the baby cry.

If it's the couple alone, they can do the chant after jumping.

Put out all the quarter candles except the south, which should be left to burn down.

Release the circle.

WATER MAGIC

Water spells are great for healing, cleansing and carrying away negativity, and for love. You can use water, rivers, the sea, the Archangel Gabriel, oils and oil burners using water.

Healing Magic Using Water

Call quarters.

Bowl of blessed water (take sea-salt and water and mix with a blessing such as: *I bless this saltwater in the name of the God and the Goddess, to remove negativity and make it fit for purpose).*

The water represents the womb of the goddess. Take a crystal or pebble you have chosen to represent someone who needs healing. Hold it to your heart and think of them healthy and well. Fill them with energy. With a statement of intent and a caveat (with harm to none, it is done), place the stone into the water.

Release quarters.

Leave the bowl out overnight, ideally in moonshine, or sunlight if daytime, or in rain.

The next day pour the water onto the ground, and reclaim the stone or bury it.

Insomnia Cure Using Water

Take blessed water and add one or two drops of lavender (if you like it – if not just use the blessed water), and sprinkle the water around the room you sleep in with the intent of removing any negativity and worries which might keep you awake. Before bed, spend some time unwinding or doing something undemanding. Ground before getting under the covers, and once in bed, focus on relaxation rather than sleep. Say a little prayer to the Goddess asking Her to guide you gently into a good night's sleep.

The sea is a great place to do rituals. In India people perform Pujas in the Ganges. I've been at a Puja ceremony at a Scottish beach where we chanted to Ganesh and drew his symbol in the sand, filling it with flower petals. We went into the sea to release what we wanted to be rid of and to send out wishes for the future. I thought it would be freezing but it was a beautiful sunny day and the ocean was warm.

EARTH MAGIC

Earth spells are good for money, a job, a home, health, and protection. You can use pentagrams, herbs, plants, knots, or tie a ribbon to a branch.

To attract Good Luck using Earth Magic

Cast a circle (outside if possible).

Call quarters – you could use the stag for the north, eagle or raven for the east, dragon or phoenix for the south, and salmon for the west.

Write your intent on a ribbon and tie it to a tree while focusing on the intent and stating it aloud.

Release the quarters and circle.

SPIRIT IS THE FIFTH ELEMENT, AND RULES THE CENTRE

The spirit is the combined essence of the four quarters and everything in the Universe. Spirit magick could be a thanksgiving for the inspiration and support you get from it. In times when things aren't going well, concentrate your thoughts on the spirit as an all-encompassing energy helping you, and seek spiritual advice from it.

TREES AND THEIR MAGICAL PROPERTIES

There are 12 to 13 full moons in a year and each has a tree associated with it. The trees listed are associated with the Celtic Moons of the Year.

The birch tree moon covers the December 24th to 20th January and represents rebirth. The birch tree is a pioneer species because it's the first tree to reappear in clear or felled areas. The birch is associated with creativity and fertility since it regenerates a forest. Birch twigs used to be hung over the cradle to protect new-born babies from evil and maladies. The Celtic name for it is Beth.

The rowan tree covers the time from January 21st to February 17th and, because of the time of year, it is associated with Brigid. Initiations are good at this time because the light is returning. Its Celtic name is Luis and it used to be planted outside people's houses to ward off evil. The berries are very bitter but have a lot of vitamin C. They can be made into preserves or mixed with apple and honey to sweeten.

The ash tree governs February 18th to March 7th. The Norse people knew it as Yggdrasil the world tree. Odin's staff was supposed to be made out of ash wood. Much of Venice is held up with ash staves. It is said to be good for prophesising, as the ash is sacred to the Druids (as well as the oak). A lot of cradles were made out of ash trees in the past because of a superstition that faeries would steal new-born children and replace them with changelings.

The alder tree governs from March 18th until April 14th. The alder flourishes along marshland and riverbanks, and it grows in damp places. It's good to use alder to improve intuition. Its roots grow into flowing water so make a pathway through the veil into another time and place. Some people thought the pipes of Pan were made of alder (others thought they were made of reeds) because alder used to be made into whistles and flutes. It has such an otherworldly sound that it was thought alder pipes could enchant people.

The willow tree time is from April 15th to May 12th. It likes its feet in the water and wet places. Willow used to be planted around cemeteries as protection (along with yew trees) – to prevent spirits from leaving there. Willow wands are good for healing rituals, and it is strongly associated with the goddess. Its Celtic name is Sailly.

The hawthorn tree governs from May 13th to June 9th. It was called Hoth by the ancient Celts. Fertility and potency is high in the land at this time and in Victorian times hawthorn became associated with faery magic.

The oak rules from June 10th to July 7th. The solstice falls during the oak's time and this is the Sun's strongest time of the year. Sacred to the Druids – indeed the name Druid is said to derive from the oak, the Celtic word for oak was Duir and means 'Men of the Oak'. Catching a falling oak leaf is supposed to bring you good luck as it symbolises strength.

The holly tree comes next from July 8th to August 4th and was thought to rule the darker part of the year. Because it is an evergreen species it is associated with the immortality of the earth. It can be used for protection; you can grow it near your home or use a holly bouquet to sprinkle blessed water as a protective blessing around the home.

The hazel period runs from August 5th to September 1st because that's when its nuts are out. It's associated with the life-force and the goddess. A pair of hazelnuts used to be handed to young couples as a blessing after they married. Y-shaped rods of hazel are used for divining or dowsing because the rod twitches when it senses water (so long as you cut one with the sap still in it).

The vine rules September 2nd to September 29th. It is associated with a bountiful harvest of grapes. Grapes and wine have long been a currency. The vine is associated with passion, indulgence and joy. It is also sacred to the dark side of the Mother Goddess. A lot of people's dark side come out when they drink red wine! Wine and grapes are good offerings to the gods.

Mistletoe was also thought of as a vine, and represents both male and female.

The ivy governs September 30th to October 27th. Known by the Celts as Gort, Ivy was used to banish negative energies and influences. You can place ivy as a barrier between yourself and whatever is ailing you or vexing you and it will absorb the negativity from whatever is harassing you. If you live on a busy road you could plant ivy in a window box to grow and absorb some of the pollution and act as a barrier between your home and the noisy dirty energy of the road. Ivy is used for binding spells too, if you had a poppet you could bind it with ivy to prevent someone from acting against you. It can also be used in handfasting to tie two people so they become one.

The reed is October 28th to November 23rd. The reed was used for flutes, clarinets, and other musical instruments. It is said that flutes made from reed were used to call the dead to the underworld, and they can be used in séances to contact spirits. If you go out in winter where reeds grow, if the wind blows the right way, it creates a haunting melody like panpipes in the hollows of the broken stems.

The elder tree governs November 24th to December 23rd, so it is in force when the solstice passes. It was used to protect against demons and malevolent spirits. It is also associated with faeries and nature spirits. The elder used to be burned slowly to create charcoal, along with the alder.

CHAPTER FIVE

BREW SOME MOONSHINE: THE ESBATS

The Esbats are the full moons of the year. Full moons are good for meeting people, making plans for the Sabbats, for planning the month ahead, and for cleansing tools and crystals. Excellent for healing magic and Goddess worship too. The Goddess is associated with the moon so all magic at this time is Goddess magick.

SOME GODDESSES FOR ESBAT MAGIC AND DEVOTION

DIANA: She is the beautiful Maiden silhouetted against the Moon. Diana is a Roman Goddess (Artemis in Greek) who is widely worshipped in modern Paganism. There are Dianic covens which generally only work with goddesses rather than male deities or the male/female polarity. She is a huntress,

51

and good for Hunter's Moon and the Grass
Moon. Farmers can pray to Diana for
protection for their animals and against
any pestilence. She is also a good Goddess
for setting goals, and setting things in
motion as her symbol is the arrow, so
Diana reminds you to aim for your desires
and fire in their direction.

THE MORRIGAN:

Triple Goddess of the Celtic pantheon,
good to call for Beaver's Moon or any
Winter Moon, and for protection magic.
She inspires great loyalty in those who
work with her and is said to often present
herself to those she feels are ready to
connect with her. She is known as a
warrior goddess, but has many aspects, and
is strongly associated with the raven.

HECATE/HEKATE:

Goddess of crossroads, the torch, and
wisdom. Hecate is another hunting
Goddess who has deerhounds by her
side. Hunter's Moon and Cold Moon
are good moons to call her. She's a very
powerful Goddess and great for protection,
transformation and enlightenment.
Known as the Goddess of Witches, she
is another Goddess often used in Wicca.

Come to Hecate for advice as to what path to follow at any particular time as she sits at the crossroads. A great Goddess to give answers, she will give an answer but sometimes you need to work it out. The truth can be given in a riddle and you may need to meditate on it. She's a good Goddess to connect with if you are having problems in your life caused by other people.

CAILLEACH: Old Celtic Crone and Wise Goddess. Call for Hunters Moon, Beaver's Moon, Cold Moon or Wolf Moon. She is often seen as the destructive aspect of nature. Her staff brings on winter and she brews up her storms in her cauldron. She is also known as Beira Queen of Winter, and the Hag. She is prominent in many Scottish folk tales and is deeply connected to the landscape there. She is the Witch of Ben Cruachan and reigns over the fierce whirlpool called the Gulf of Corryvreckan.

BRIGID: Imbolc Goddess and British Goddess Maiden aspect. Good for Snow Moon magic and Worm Moon. I invite Brigid in every year to bless the house at Imbolc, and she's a go-to Goddess for healing. She is

	also associated with the arts and has a long history in Britain and Ireland.
OSTARA:	Grass Moon, Goddess of Fertility and Spring.
ARIANRHOD:	Goddess of love and fertility, good for Flower Moon magic. Used a lot in Wicca as a focus to channel energy.
APHRODITE:	Greek Goddess of Love and Beauty. Ideal for Grass Moon or Flower Moon or Rose/Strawberry Moon. Born from the sea, she is associated with pearls and dolphins, but also the rose. A good Goddess to call for love magick, beauty and new relationships, and to increase the joys of womanhood, or of life in general.
DEMETER:	Greek Goddess of the Harvest and Mother of Persephone. Good for Buck Moon, Sturgeon Moon and Harvest Moon. She can be called to represent the Mother Goddess, and connected to by meditating in a field of grain or barley. If you are looking for something, you can call on Demeter to find it for you. Demeter found her own daughter who was being held by Hades (there are other versions of this story too), and made the bargain with Hades that he would release her daughter for part of the year. You can pray to

Demeter for healing, especially if you have lost someone. It's nice to have sunflowers around or some kind of field flower when you call on Her. She is another Goddess commonly used in witchcraft, especially at the harvest festivals.

LET US NOT FORGET THE GODS

The gods are usually associated with the sun and the wheel of the year, and being the consort to the goddess.

CERNUNNOS:

Also known as Herne and the Green Man of the Forest. He is a Celtic god, guardian of the wild, and watches over the day to day happenings in nature and the animals of the forest. He is a good consort to call for Brigid. A magical experience Garry had when he was 17 years old, was one cold morning at the bottom of the treeline on Ben Vorlich, a stag appeared in the clearing and stood staring him. He could see its breath in the air, and it was his first moment of connection with Cernunnos, and he has used him lots of times since, and keeps that image in mind when invoking him. Herne is good for protection or strength, or to bring any plans to fruition – which he is good for because of his strength.

PAN: The Greek God of the Herd. Pan is a God of Strength and Fertility. He chases the nymphs around the woodlands. After cornering one nymph, she turned herself into syrinx (a flute), he picked her up, played her and this became his instrument. He has a tricky side so you've got to watch, he plays pranks or sometimes your ritual won't work out. There is a statue at Mearns Kirk Hospital in East Renfrewshire named Peter Pan where the figure looks more like the God Pan than the fictional character. The statue plays the flute, and has one foot on a tortoise (associated with the God Pan) and another foot on a hare!

ODIN: The supreme power of Norse culture. He has two ravens, Hugin and Munin, who are his messengers. Hugin is Old Norse meaning 'thought' and Munin is Old Norse meaning 'mind'. The ravens flew all over the world and took messages back to Odin – perhaps that's where George RR Martin got his idea for three-eyed ravens that act as messengers in his medieval fantasy *Game of Thrones*? Odin also hung from the tree Yggdrasil for three days and there developed the Norse alphabet. You could also call Odin to ask him to help you towards a path of truth, or for fulfilment, as he has can see through everything and everybody. Near Samhain is a good time to think of Odin. You can call Him to help solve your problems. People used to think finding a black feather was a message from Odin saying your prayers would be answered.

ZEUS: Zeus is the great leader of the Gods and demi-Gods of Mount Olympus. Also known as Jupiter and Jove. He watches down on humanity, he is a great benevolent God but not one to be crossed either. He is the father of gods in the Greek and Roman pantheons, and a Sky God associated with lightning bolts and the eagle. A good God to call to send strength to others (or wrath!). He is a God of great abundance and fertility so can be called for success in all endeavours and for great things. In the past, rulers may have prayed to Zeus to win wars and conquer lands.

THE PANTHEONS

The many pantheons parallel each other and the gods and goddesses in them are sometimes similar – harvest gods and fertility gods and dark gods, but the mythology and details vary from one pantheon to another. Famous pantheons are:

Greek: Zeus, Hera, Poseidon, Demeter, Athena, Apollo, Artemis, Ares, Hephaestus, Aphrodite, Hermes, Dionysus.

Roman: Jupiter, Juno, Minerva, Neptune, Venus, Mars, Apollo, Diana, Vulcan, Vesta, Mercury, Ceres.

Celtic: Danu, Dagda, Aengus, Lugh, the Morrigan, Brigid, Belenus, Toutatis, Camulos, Taranis, Cernunnos, Ogmios, Grannus, Epona, Eriu.

Egyptian: Osiris, Isis, Horus, Seth, Ptah, Ra, Hathor, Anubis, Thoth, Bastet, Amon.

Norse: Odin, Balder, Bragi, Forseti, Freya, Heimdallr, Loki, Thor.

This is by no means an exhaustive list of the gods. Some people favour working within one pantheon, but we both work across them.

THE MOONS

The moons were named in North America in the early 20th century and drew on a mixture of British farming lore and Native American traditions.

The Hunter's Moon (Oct): This Moon is connected to hunting. The leaves are falling, the corn has been cut, the animals are vulnerable to being seen. Deer and hares are more visible and can't hide among trees and grain, and the fields are clear for horses to ride through. This is a time for healing magic because the winter is coming, and also for preparing for Samhain.

The Beaver Moon (Nov): The Americans called it this because they set the traps for beaver pelts at this time before the ice froze, as they needed to go under the water to set the traps. It is the month of the US Thanksgiving, and a good time for thanks giving for everyone.

The Cold Moon (Dec): This is the month when the longest night comes and the days become longer after that. It is also the month of the most festivities, in older times people would eat what had to be eaten from the harvest. You could light a fire outside to celebrate the return of the Sun and make plans for Yule (if the moon comes before Yule).

Although the ancestors and what went before are remembered at Samhain, the Cold Moon and Yule are also a good time to remember what has gone before, and people who have affected our lives positively. It's a time of wishes, so make wishes, and be grateful for what has been.

> INTENT: To send well wishes and thanks for those who have gone who have had a good influence on your life, and send out magic for other people to come into your life who will bring positive things your way.

> Bless candles with your intents (many and of various colours to bring light to the dark month – the more colours the better since winter has fewer natural colours so you are bringing both light and colour into your life). You are both banishing negativity and bringing positivity with these candles. You can anoint them to remove negativity (I go from the centre to the ends, if it's a taper), and by lighting it you empower it with positivity. Think about your intents as you anoint, as you light the candles state your intent: ie. *I give thanks for any blessings coming my way OR I give thanks to … for … this and that.* Thank for things you wish for as well as things which have already come to pass which are good. With this, you are both sending out thanks and sending out your wishes for the future.

The Wolf Moon (Jan): Given this name because hungry wolves used to circle small villages in winter looking for vulnerable livestock. Wolves which usually stayed in the hills would come nearer settlements. A good time for protection magic for yourself, your home, your family and friends.

The Snow or Hunger Moon (Feb): So named because there was less food. In the modern context, it's good time to start a diet or fitness plan because the year is progressing and the seeds you sow in the early part of the year blossom in the later part. Now is the time to sow some magickal seeds you'd like to see come to fruition later.

The Worm Moon (March): The time of the year the earth in the Northern Hemisphere starts to thaw, you see robins again (last seen in December) because they are looking for worms. Called the Worm Moon because you see worm casts on the ground as they become more active. This is the start of spring. The ravens breed. The crows pair up and nest in March. A time for reflection on how balanced your life is, where your priorities lie and how you're spending your time. Also, a good time for sowing seeds for the future and casting magic for a desired outcome in the near future.

> Choose a tree and ask for its permission to help your magic.

> Select a supple thin young branch and, without cutting or tearing it, bend it gently around the trunk or a larger branch with your intent in mind, and tie it in place as it is snaked round the tree with a cord so it will grow in that position. Bless the tree and thank it.

The Grass or Pink Moon (April): Time of wildflowers and daffodils, buds swell and burst on trees, the grass grows again – hence Grass Moon. Magically, it's a time for things happening, colour is returning, the landscape is greener and less barren. Good for love magic or abundance, and meeting new friends and partners of all kinds.

The Flower Moon (May): Blazes of spring colour are everywhere. A time of birth, young birds hatch. Good magic for the May Moon would include celebrations of the Sun, and magic to achieve things – because the Sun has power at this time.

The Strawberry Moon, Rose Moon or Full Hay Moon (June): Named after ripening strawberries and blooming roses. A time of fertility. Young stags grow their first antlers. Good magic could be thanks for the abundance in your life or sending blessings to others as both the Sun and Moon are strong together. Magic to heal relationships, to bring people together, for unity and for harmony are special to this moon. A celebration of light before the dark half of the year starts to come in is appropriate now too.

Optional circle and quarters.

Select an oak tree, take a ribbon or clootie (old Scottish word meaning cloth), choose a branch you like, then, and while focused on your intent, tie your ribbon in a knot round the branch. Push a crystal –

citrine ideally but any crystal is good – into the soil beneath the tree as a blessing and thanks.

Release circle and quarters.

The Buck Moon (**July**): The antlers of the stags are covered in velvet before hardening for the rutting season. There is an abundance of butterflies around. A good time for Faery Magic.

Cast a circle.

Call quarters – elements or elementals or power animals.

Burn incense – a light flowery incense like jasmine, rose, ylang-ylang, lavender. Have flowers and libations as a salute to the faery realm and as an offering. Drink a libation and offer the rest to the faeries. Light candles or a small fire.

Depending on the area/habitat, call on the faeries of the woods/or the spirits of the ocean, or the faeries of the garden:

I invite the good spirits and faery folk of this sacred place to join with me/us and bring harmony and happiness with you, as we offer gifts and blessing to you. Hail and welcome.

Sit with them for a while, meditate, or pathwork with them – imagine yourself with them, rest into the warmth of their presence. Or you could send some healing magic for the earth – such as if trees were being cut down somewhere you might want to send those responsible second thoughts. This could be done by having one candle (unlit) represent the thing which is happening then make a statement about what you want to halt, light it quickly then extinguish it with some water to halt it. Add the caveat 'with harm to none, it is done.'

Give thanks for the faeries 'Go if you must, stay if you will, thanks for joining us/me, hail and farewell.' Release quarters and circle.

The Sturgeon Moon (August): Also known as the Mackerel Moon due to the shoals of mackerel coming into shallow water to be fished. A good time to fix things and make sure things are in working order, and for magick to solve problems.

The Harvest Moon (Sept): The Harvest Moon allowed the farmers to work later as the darkness was starting to come in earlier, so they could stay out to gather crops. A good time for community as everyone used to get together to help out, the old saying 'make hay while the Sun shines' comes to mind. Make incense, gather wood for fires. Good magick could involve getting rid of the old and in with the new in preparation for winter, and to bring about balance.

Optional circle and quarters.

One black and one white cord rope symbolising light and dark and balance. Focus on your intent (whatever that is) and tie both cords together in the middle firmly saying your intent out loud. Pulling them together so they create a perfect cross. Keep it somewhere safe after the ritual. This can also be used as a binding spell.

Release quarters and circle.

CHAPTER SIX

THE WHEEL OF THE YEAR GOES ROUND AND ROUND

THE WHEEL

The Wheel of the Year is a celebration of the seasons and the cycle of life, death and rebirth. Some Pagan celebrations coincide with Christian – such as Yuletide/ Christmas and Easter/Ostara. Some of the other Pagan festivals also have their Christian counterparts – All Hallow's Eve (Samhain), Loafmass (Lammas) and Applemass (Autumn Equinox), Candlemass (Imbolc), but these are still celebrated by modern Pagans, whereas I'm uncertain whether Christians still celebrate them.

THE SABBATS

Samhain

When I was a kid, I loved it when the nights started drawing in and that autumnal Halloween scent rose up in the air. Our school celebrated it with paper lanterns and turnip carving and dressing up, and my parents always threw a neighbourhood Halloween party with games, like treacle scones and dooking (bobbing) for apples. As children, both Garry and I were fascinated by witches, ghosts and magic, and attracted by mysterious things. In ancient times, at this time of year, people spent their time indoors in the evenings to get out of the chill and because not so much work was done in the hours of darkness. Entertainment switched to the indoors and storytelling round the fire, and these shared legends, myths and spiritual fables form the backbone of many cultures.

Samhain is a fire festival and the gateway to the darkest part of the year. It is also the Celtic/Pagan New Year and start of winter, and the most celebrated time for witches and Pagans. This is a good time for rites for letting things go, moving on, or for lighting candles to people who have passed away. It is a time of reflection on the past year and the lessons you've learned. The veil between the worlds is at its thinnest so welcome the spirits of your ancestors into your home. Gods or goddesses to call could be Hecate or Persephone. Call the ancestors too, and make offerings of food and wine, wish them peace, tell them how much they are missed and revered, and bid farewell.

A Hecate Samhain Ritual

Set a Hecate altar in the centre of the circle, representing the crossroads – with something to symbolise the Moon (a crystal ball/white sphere, or statue, red wine and crescent shaped cakes for after the ritual).

You can memorise a small calling rather than read out a lengthy one for a deity, although it's about your preference.

As this is New Year, you could do a ritual for healing – letting an illness pass away into the darkness and the person be reborn. Collect all darkness and release it.

Cast circle.

Call quarters.

Light a candle (black or red or purple) or three candles (white, red, black), and call:

Hecate, Dark Queen of the Crossroads and paths,

Light-bearer, Goddess of the Moon and magic,

Lady of the Underworld,

We call upon you to witness our rite and protect our circle.

Hail and welcome!

State the reason you are there. Choose one thing for everyone to focus on – so if you're there to heal one member of the group or yourself – make a statement about it, such as: *Hecate please send healing to....who has been... and dissolve this bad luck/ill health etc.*

Raise some energy – the hoof and horn chant or the river is flowing chant are possible ways – until the energy is built up and then release it by swinging arms up and letting the energy go.

Hoof and Horn, Hoof and Horn, All that dies shall be reborn.

Corn and Grain, Corn and Grain, All that falls shall rise again.

OR

The river is flowing; flowing and growing. The river is flowing down to the sea, Mother carry me, your child I will always be, Mother carry me, down to the sea.

Male holds the chalice of red wine and the female puts in the tip of the athame and blesses the wine in the name of Hecate and draws an invoking earth pentacle over the wine and cakes. Share the wine and cakes around each member and leave some for an offering. When passing round you could say:

From me to thee blessed be.

Thank Hecate for joining and overseeing the rite. Say: *Stay if you will, go if you must.*

Release the quarters and circle.

The circle is open but unbroken, may the Goddess be always in your heart.

Put the rest of the offerings outside after the ritual.

YULE

This is about moving from dark to light. Yule is a time of rebirth, the Sun is reborn and starts its journey to the midsummer heights. It's a good time for a celebration of life and rebirth and giving thanks and gifts. A time for sharing with family and friends and sowing the seeds of a good future. Make plans and resolutions. Leave all negativity behind and bring on the good times. Gods for this time are... Santa! Or Herne. Take evergreen trees into the house to celebrate new life. Garry's gran used to make the kids go collect bits of greenery and holly from hedgerows to bring in for good luck and to decorate the Christmas dinner table.

IMBOLC

This is Brigid's celebration. House blessings are good at this time. This is the first spring festival, and it represents new growth and awakening. The Earth stretches fingers through the ground, and the first flowers come through.

Imbolc means 'in the belly' or 'ewe milk' referring to the Earth Goddess and spring lambs lying in the bellies of their mothers. Christians gave it the evocative name of Candlemass. Light lots of candles to bring back in the light. It's a good time for giving offerings to Brigid.

Example House Blessing for Imbolc

Spring-clean the house.

Cast circle, call quarters.

Starting at the front door, go round widdershins (anticlockwise) with saltwater sprinkling it and saying: *By salt and sea, of harm stay free.*

Return to the front door and light incense, and go round your home deosil (clockwise) wafting the smoke and saying: *By fire and air, bless this place.*

Return to your altar, light a candle for Brigid and call:

Lovely Brigid, Goddess of spring, bright fiery Maiden, Goddess of the Land, share your gifts, and bless this home with your presence. Hail and Welcome!

State your intent.

Give an offering of tea with honey.

Give thanks, release quarters and circle.

OSTARA/VERNAL EQUINOX

A time of birth, everything is coming alive, new buds opening on the trees. The young Goddess is becoming older. The birds nest, and flowers become more abundant. Hares run over the land. It's a good time to welcome the Sun and the warmth. Associated with the Goddess Ostara – who is a Green Goddess and protector of animals and young birds. A time of perfect balance between day and night.

BELTANE

The Maiden has grown into a young woman who mates with the god. A fertile time, a time of fruition. Love magic, handfasting, abundance magic – the growth is strong from Beltane until Midsummer for all sorts of abundance magic. This is the Celtic start of summer and a time of creation, so do magic for things you want to create in your life. It is also a time of enhancement so if you have particular plans, use this time to get the best from them. Gods and goddesses – Pan, Diana.

Goddess Diana, Lady of the Moon and the hunt,
Inspiration for new directions,
bringing dreams to fruition,
Goddess of goals searched for,
please bless this circle with your divine presence.

We both shared a spiritual time on the Isle of Arran at Beltane a few years ago at a friend's handfasting. There were about 40 people, and some of us shared a beautiful house overlooking the bay. There were workshops for broom-making, drumming, and sound therapy. We had a bonfire and burned a wickerman called Steve!

MIDSUMMER

The longest day of the year, with growth at its highest point. Midsummer is an old religious fire festival among the Celts, Germanic people, and the Scandinavians. It's also associated with the Oak and Holly King myth. The Oak King has reached the top of his reign, since he has been on the throne since Yule, and the Holly King fights him and takes his crown and sends him into the earth until Yule returns. The Holly King rules the dark time of the year. Gods and goddesses – the Green Man (Herne of the Hunt) and Demeter are good to call here.

LAMMAS

The first harvest festival. Harvest festivals were common even in Christian Britain, and the historian and writer Ron Hutton documents numerous examples of harvest rituals from all over the country dating from the 16th century. Lammas is a time for reaping what you've sown and of plenty. Good for planning, saving and thinking about what you can give back. A time of sharing and breaking bread, community and family. Lugh, Herne and Demeter are good gods to work with now.

AUTUMN EQUINOX

The opposite of the vernal equinox. Darkness takes over from this time onwards, and this is the waning part of the year. The second harvest, sometimes called Applemass, after the apple harvest. A time of community, settling down, relaxing, reaping what you've sown. Gods – Demeter and Pan.

CHAPTER SEVEN

A LITTLE HISTORY

Witchcraft became a capital offence in England in 1542 and in Scotland in 1563. This was extended in 1649 to include death for blasphemy and the worship of false gods. In 1735 these were replaced with The Witchcraft Act which said witchcraft effectively didn't exist and anyone who claimed to be one could instead be charged as a con artist (fortune-tellers, mediumship, etc). This remained in place in Britain until 1951.

Four thousand 'witches' are thought to have perished in Scotland during the witch hunts, and half that number in England. There are many infamous incidents such as the Pendle Witches, the Paisley Witches, and the Scottish witch-hunts of 1597 and 1661-1662. Many thousands of people died across Europe too.

DR JOHN DEE (July 1527–Dec 1608)

From the court of Elizabeth I, Dee was a mathematician, the Queen's advisor, an astrologer and occultist. He made predictions based on communing with angels and developed a system of magick called Enochian, which filtered down through the centuries, through the ceremonial magick of the Victorian era, and elements of it can be seen in modern Wicca (the Watchtowers, for example).

KING JAMES I/VI (1556–1625)

The son of Mary Queen of Scots became known as the witch-hunter King of Scotland, and subsequently of England too. He was obsessed with witches and wrote an influential book called *Daemonologie* which resulted in an upsurge in persecution. He even attended some tortures personally.

SALEM (1692)

Witch-hunts had come into disrepute by the end of the 17th century but in 1692 A group of Puritan girls in colonial Massachusetts kicked off a panic which had 200 people accused of witchcraft and fraternising with the devil. Men accused rivals to steal their property, women accused neighbours they disliked, and it finally ended in shame a year later with twenty people executed, and more dead or imprisoned. Stacey Schiff's book *The Witches* is an excellent account of what happened.

THE HERMETIC ORDER OF THE GOLDEN DAWN

Founded by William Robert Woodman, William Wynn Westcott, and Samuel Liddell Mathers, this was an influential and secret magical order based in Great Britain. The founders were freemasons and the order had a hierarchical structure, although women were allowed in. They practiced Kabbalistic magic. Mathers also translated the old magical text *The Key of Solomon* and established temples to Egyptian Gods in England. The Golden Dawn was a precursor to modern witchcraft and paganism. It had many prominent members such as Bram Stoker, WB Yeats, Aleister Crowley and Sherlock Holmes author Sir Arthur Conan Doyle.

ALEISTER CROWLEY (Oct 1875–Dec 1947)

Crowley was an occultist and ceremonial magician, author and member of The Golden Dawn, although he moved away to form his own sect. He associated himself with the number 666 from the Book of Revelations, used mind-altering drugs and became addicted to heroin. He also played a big role in bringing back witchcraft and magick to the Western world. Gerald Gardner drew on Crowley's work in the early years of Wicca before departing down a path of his own. The Wiccan ceremony of *Drawing Down the Moon* owes a lot to Crowley. He became a cult figure associated with free love and debauchery, and ran a commune in Sicily, but was deported from Italy for depravity, and dubbed the 'wickedest man in England' by the press. Nonetheless he heavily influenced magickal practices, and the Goddess worship movement which came afterwards. He used ritual structures from The Golden Dawn, who themselves adapted a lot from the Freemasons. Crowley features on the cover of the Beatles album *Sergeant Pepper's Lonely Hearts Club Band*. Jimmy Page, the Led Zeppelin guitarist, bought Crowley's Bolskine House on Loch Ness after his death.

GERALD GARDNER (1884–1964)

Known as the father of modern witchcraft. His coven was the Brickle Wood Coven in England and he was an Initiate of The New Forest Coven. Today, Gardnerian witches follow the rules of his Book of Shadows, and ideally their lineage should be descended from his coven – which means to gain the Gardnerian pedigree you need to trace your Wiccan heritage directly back to the Gardner's coven, ie. be initiated by someone who can trace their heritage back. After the repeal of the witchcraft act in the UK in 1951, Gardner became public and published articles about witchcraft. This caused a falling out with his pupil Doreen Valiente. Access to Gardner's Book of Shadows and his practices is traditionally restricted, depending on the stage of initiation.

DOREEN VALIENTE (Jan 1922–Sep 1999)

A member of the Brickle Wood Coven, who forged a new coven after a spat with Gerald Gardner over publicity. She took one of Gardener's circle members to become her High Priest. She was also an author and studied the Golden Dawn for years before meeting Gardner. She is credited with the *Charge of the Goddess* (although this was also Crowley's work, and even others before him). She was a huge influence on the development of Wicca in the modern world.

ALEX SANDERS

Gardnerian witch and founder of Alexandrian witchcraft, which is similar to Gardnerian tradition except that no descent from the New Forest coven is required to initiate. He also added more ceremonial aspects into Gardnerian Wicca.

STUART AND JANET FERRAR

He was an Alexandrian witch initiated by Maxine Sanders (Alex Sander's wife), and an author. He and Janet had a coven in Ireland. His books were influential and showed the general public altars, and practices that were detailed. They specified how to conduct a ritual. Janet carried on Stuart's lineage after his death, taking Gavin Bone as her High Priest.

TYPES OF PRACTICE

There are many different types of pagan practice, but a few examples are:

Wicca

Wicca emerged in the mid 20th century from Gerald Gardner, Doreen Valiente and others. Key elements of Wicca include Goddess worship, following the wheel of the year, adherence to the *Wiccan Rede*, and practices such as *Drawing Down the Moon* (which is when you draw the energy of the Moon Goddess into the circle). In Gardnerian and Alexandrian Wicca, there are three degrees of initiation. Other Wiccan paths include Celtic, which focuses on Celtic deities, and Dianic (female-centred, Goddess worship).

Druid

Modern Druidry was reformed around the same time as Wicca, but Druids are an ancient tradition in Britain. Julius Caesar documented much of the Druid activity in Britain and Gaul. They were the doctors, the priestly cast, and, as Holy Men, they were accepted in the upper echelons of society. They served tribal elders and rulers, and led religious ceremonies. Their last stronghold was in Anglesey in Wales. Later when Christianity came to Britain, the Druids finally gave way. The resurgence of

Druidry began in the mid 20th century. The Druid path is about gaining wisdom from nature and ancient stories that were told – like the story of Taliesin, which, drawing on Celtic folklore, is about a young bard who travels through the countryside becoming the animals he encounters, to know their wisdom. The Druids' main governing body is OBOD. There are three initiations to become a fully-fledged Druid, which are Bardic, Ovate and Druid.

Shamanism

This is a path where people connect with nature and the spirits and elements around them through astral travel, the use of herbs and plants, and totem animals.

Ceremonial

This is a brand of magick that works chiefly with the tree of life, with angels, with tarot and astrology. It uses circles, quarters and invocations and is connected to Crowley, to the Order of the Golden Dawn and old magical texts.

Norse/Heathen

Based on the Viking sagas of old and the gods these people worshipped, like Freya, Odin and Loki. The Norse were highly cultured and spiritual, and had a strong code of honour.

Sumerian

This started in Mesopotamia and is thought to be the oldest religion of that region. It dates back to the early Bronze Age and was a civilisation that existed alongside ancient Egypt (another branch of practice that has been around for a very long time and has enjoyed a resurgence). The Sumerian Goddess Inanna is one of the earliest recorded deities. She later became known as Ishtar when she was worshipped by the Babylonians, Akkadians and Assyrians. The earliest known author was the poet Enheduanna who was a High Priestess of Inanna. She wrote poems, hymns and dedications to the goddess, some of which still exist and can be read.

Eclectic Path

The eclectic makes their own way through Paganism and witchcraft without adhering to one tradition or pantheon necessarily. The eclectic practices Paganism in a way that feels right for them and their purpose, taking from different traditions as they wish.

MYSTICAL PLACES IN SCOTLAND

Scotland has a rich history and abundance of legend and folklore. It is full of magickal places, Pictish stones, old graveyards, ruined castles and ancient sites. We both love visiting places of historical interest and have been on magickal trips with friends to Arran, Orkney, the standing stones at Kilmartin Glen, and other places to do ritual and just have a holiday with a spiritual flavour.

Orkney – Garry performed a handfasting at the Stones of Stenness here. The Orkney Islands have many Neolithic attractions such as the Maeshowe Tomb, the Standing Stones of Stenness and the Ring of Brodgar. Prehistoric civilisation in Orkney is one of the oldest in the world, dating back 5000 years. There are the burial cairns – the tomb of the otters and the tomb of the eagles, and Skara Brae – a settlement which was discovered after a huge storm. The Ring of Brodgar was known as the Temple of the Sun, the Stones of Stenness as the Temple of the Moon. When the Vikings came in the 9th century, they adopted the Ring of Brodgar for the worship of Odin. My great-grandmother was Orcadian, and the graveyards in North Ronaldsay and Sanday Island hold lots of my ancestors.

Isle of Lewis – Home to the stunning 5000-year-old Callandish standing stones which were a focus for rituals during the Bronze Age. They are astrologically aligned and nicknamed 'The Stonehenge of Scotland'. An enigmatic figure known as *The Shining One* is said to walk through the stones at dawn every Midsummer's morning.

Rosslyn Chapel – This mystical 15th century chapel, just outside Edinburgh, features in the Dan Brown novel *The Da Vinci Code*. Conspiracies about the chapel have divided historians for many years, as have the significance of the Pagan symbols within the church. It has been connected to the Knights Templar, and there are stories that the chapel is haunted.

Glencoe – Beautiful Glencoe has a history of murder and betrayal, where the Clan MacDonald were massacred by the Campbells for failing to swear fealty to the new King in 1691. The spirits of the dead are said to wander there, and some people claim to have heard ghostly pipes playing in the glen.

Edinburgh – There are Merlin myths all over Scotland (and the rest of the UK too) and one of them is that the dormant volcano at the bottom of Edinburgh's Royal Mile was the original seat of Camelot – the romanticised Kingdom of Sir Arthur and his Knights. Today Edinburgh is known among Harry Potter fans as one of the inspirations of JK Rowling's books and some of the cobbled curved streets look not dissimilar to Diagon Alley, and the dirty stairwells and 'closes' are very Nocturne Alley. There are of plenty Harry Potter shops and cafes where Rowling wrote the books, there is also Greyfriar's Kirk graveyard with Tom Riddle's grave (a real grave). Sherlock Holmes creator Arthur Conan Doyle was from Edinburgh, and apparently Holmes was based on one of his Edinburgh teachers. Doyle was fascinated by spiritualism and was a member of the Victorian magical society, The Order of the Golden Dawn.

Corryvreckan – The Cauldron of Corryvreckan is one of the largest natural whirlpools in the world, and is sacred to the Cailleach. Legend has it that the pool was stirred by the Queen of Winter, who lives high in the peak of Schiehallion. Another legend about Corryvreckan is that a Scandinavian prince plunged to his death in its depths after trying to anchor his boat there.

Kilmartin Glen – A beautiful landscape. Sites here including standing stones, stone circles and the Iron Age hillfort Dunadd where the ancient Kings were crowned.

Iona – Iona is where many of the old Scottish kings are buried. St Columba, who converted much of Britain to Christianity, settled here in the 6th century. But its connections are not only Christian, they are also Pagan, and Iona has plenty of stories of rituals, fairies and ghosts. It has a lovely abbey built by the Viking Raghnall in 1200 AD, and an old nunnery. St Oran's grave is also here. Legend has it that when he first landed on the island, Oran suggested that he should be buried alive as a living sacrifice to the island which would be sanctified by this. Columba agreed and Oran was buried. After three days the grave was opened up and Columba and his monks were horrified to find Oran still alive. As he spoke the words, 'There is no such great wonder in death, nor is hell what it has been described', Columba ordered, 'Earth, earth!' on Oran's eyes 'lest he further blab'! And so, Oran was re-buried alive. The composer Mendelssohn said of Iona, *"When in some future time I shall sit in a madly crowded assembly with music and dancing round me, and the wish arises to retire into the loneliest loneliness, I shall think of Iona."* My great-grandfather was raised here before being conscripted into the First World War.

Pictish Art – There are many gems from the Pictish Kingdom all over Scotland, from Fowlis Wester to the Duppling Cross inside St Serf's Church in Dunning with its beautiful 12th-century square tower. There is also the Meigle Museum which has a collection of Pictish stones, and St Vigeans Museum with 38 stones. There is also Aberlemno which is home to four stones in what appear to be at or near their original locations: three along the roadside, and one in the churchyard. They range from early incised symbols on standing stones, to elaborate, carved Christian cross slabs. The churchyard stone may be the single most famous Pictish stone, depicting a famous battle against Anglo-Saxons. There are many more such as Maiden's Stone which is still clearly marked, and Sueno's Stone – tall at 7metres. Burghead Fort is one of the largest sites, and there are various artefacts and carvings displayed at Tarbet Discovery Centre at Portmahomack. The Picts were great sculptors and there is a Pictish Trail which takes in a lot of the art and sights.

Arran – The whole island is magically beautiful, and Machrie Moor, with its great standing stones set in a tranquil ground surrounded by distant hills, is one of our favourite places. Just off Arran is the Holy Isle which now has a Buddhist retreat where people can stay and do mindfulness courses and other workshops. The island is also a nature reserve for Eriskay ponies, Saanen goats and Soay sheep. There is also a healing well and the hermit cave of 6th century monk St Molaise on the Holy Isle.

Loch Ness – Loch Ness is near the city of Inverness, as well as the prehistoric Clava Cairns and standing stones, and the battlefield Culloden.

Loch Ness never freezes over, not even in the winter, and on icy days you can see steam rising from the loch's dark surface. The loch contains more water than all the lakes of England and Wales combined so there's room enough for the water beast known as the Loch Ness Monster – first chronicled in the 5th century by St Columba.

But there's more to Scottish mythological creatures than the Loch Ness Monster. Kelpies were said to live in lochs and transform into beautiful horses or women to try to attract people to them, but if someone were to mount them, they would drag them into the water to drown. There are also Selkies – which are also called the Seal People – which can turn into humans. There is a story about a man who one morning noticed a Selkie coming out of the water, removing her seal skin and turning into a woman. The man sneaked down and stole the Selkie's skin and took it to his cottage and locked it in a chest. The Selkie pleaded with the man to give her the skin back to which he replied that she would get it back one day if she married him. They married and had three children; the children were young when he went out to sea one day forgetting he had left the key to the chest out. The Selkie took the key, recovered her skin and returned to the sea leaving them behind. Other Scottish mythological creatures are Brownies, which are fairies who do favours for farmers, who would leave out offerings for them.

Aberfoyle Fairy Hill – Robert Kirk was a Minister in Balquhidder who moved to Aberfoyle and took daily walks on Doune Hill – which was next to his church. He said there he met fairy people, and went on to write a book about it called *'The Secret Commonwealth of Elves, Fauns and Fairies.'* The two castes of fairies he documented were called the Seelie and the Unseelie. Then one day his body was found on the hill, and the story went that he was taken away by fairies and his spirit led away to become Minister of the Fae.

Lots of Pagans work with the Fae, also called The Shining ones or Sidhe. I've asked for help in the garden, to protect the animals and birds that live in it. To work with them you might want to meditate to connect and ask for their help. You can ask them to help you find something for example. Fairies are very protective spirits, but also sometimes mischievous. Magick with them is potentially tricky, and they are not to be crossed.

Skye – The mountainous Isle of Skye is romantic and beautiful, with waterfalls which are said to be healing. It is home to Loch Coruisk where Kelpies are said to live. Skye, like a lot of Scotland, has a strong belief in faeries dating back to prehistoric times. Skye's fairy lore is abundant – the Fairy Glen and Fairy Pools, at the foot of the Black Cuillins, are thought to be one of their homes.

CHAPTER EIGHT

SPELLICIOUS FOOD

SAMHAIN: PUMPKIN SOUP
(*Serve with Garlic Bread or Croutons*)

Take a medium to large pumpkin that can be used as a Jack o' Lantern after the soup. Remove the seeds and pith. Scrape the meat of the pumpkin out for the soup. Fry a large onion and garlic in oil. Add plain flour once the onion is translucent to make a roux. Add a pinch of mace. Add water and stock (2 pints for a medium to large pumpkin), chop up pumpkin flesh small and add to the pot. Bring to the boil, add two large potatoes and let simmer for 40 minutes. Then add a tablespoon of tomato puree, and bouquet garner of herbs (or miscellaneous Italian herbs like rosemary, basil). Allow the soup to simmer down until it starts to caramelise at the bottom without sticking. Then add more stock (a pint and a half with this recipe). Then liquidise or blend. Keep it simmering until you have the consistency you want. Season with salt and pepper, and (if you like) serve with double cream drizzled on top.

YULE: YULE VEGETABLE MEDLEY
AND MULLED WINE

2 large parsnips, 4 large carrots, 2 celery sticks, half a medium turnip all peeled and chunked. Put vegetable stock (¼ pint) in the bottom of a baking tray to help steam the veg. Add olive oil and a pinch of mace and drizzle honey over the top. Season with salt and pepper and cover the baking tray with tinfoil. Place in the oven on a medium heat for 45 minutes. Once cooked uncover and sprinkle with pine nuts.

Mulled Wine: Take two bottles of red wine and pour into a pot and put on a low heat just to warm it, add two cinnamon sticks, sliced ginger, the juice of one lemon, the juice of two oranges and some juniper berries. Do not boil or the alcohol content will reduce. This recipe also works with non-alcoholic red wine.

IMBOLC: SCOTCH BROTH WITH HAGGIS
(and Vegetarian Version)

Soak broth mix for a minimum of 12 hours, chop a large sweet onion, heat with butter until soft, add finely cubed carrots (2 large) and turnip. For carnivores: add a lamb flank and 4 pints of lamb stock. For vegetarians: add 4 pints of vegetable stock. Chop up 6 medium potatoes and add, let simmer, adding the strained broth mix. Let simmer for 1 hr 15 minutes adding stock as required. Add 3 bay leaves, and finally chopped parsley. Towards the end of cooking, you can add a tin of haggis or vegetarian haggis to make the broth extra hearty for the winter. Serve with crusty bread.

OSTARA: OSTARA KEGERIE
(*Smoked Fish with Rice and Eggs*)

Add long grain rice to a pot of boiling vegetable stock and cook for 15 minutes then drain and add a dessert spoonful of turmeric. In a separate pan, fry up an onion with garlic in butter until soft, add two fillets of smoked haddock (chopped) and a touch of mace. Add black pepper and butter. Boil three large eggs (hen or duck) until hard boiled. Chop a dozen cherry tomatoes and mix through the rice, along with a handful of chopped chives. Add curry powder to the fish when it is cooking. Put rice in a bowl, lay the fish on top of it, slice the boiled eggs and place round the edges of the dish. Add chopped parsley as a garnish.

VEGAN OSTARA STIR-FRY

Chop up sweet potato, butternut squash, carrots, onions, garlic and put in a pan with olive oil and butter. Fry up until al dente, add tins of chopped tomatoes and mangetout. Add cooked basmati rice and vegetable stock and simmer until stock is boiled off, and serve.

BELTANE: FRENCH BEANS PROVENCAL

Sweat off two large onions in butter and olive oil, add three chopped cloves of garlic, two tins of chopped tomatoes, some tarragon, vegetable stock (a pint), reduce down until it is like a thick soup, then add fresh French beans. Cook all until al-dente (maybe 6 mins). Add tomato puree to thicken, and an optional drizzle of honey at the end to lift the sweetness. Garnish with fresh coriander. This could be served with a baked potato.

MIDSUMMER: PASTA PUTTENESCA

Take one bag of penne pasta and boil until al dente in water with a dessertspoon of turmeric and a touch of mace. Have a separate pan with butter and olive oil simmering, place the pasta into it and coat the pasta, and add paprika (2 teaspoons). Set aside and cover to stop it drying out while you make the sauce. One bulb of garlic chopped, a large onion, heat and soften these in olive oil, add three tins of chopped tomatoes, fresh basil and coriander and sage and rosemary. Add in a pint of vegetable stock and reduce down, add a dozen pitted sliced olives and 15 caper berries (chopped) and 6 small gherkins (the pickled kind). You can add roast vegetables or chicken or seafood to this as you wish. Heat the pasta up and mix the sauce through.

LAMMAS – DHAL WITH FRAGRANT RICE

Boil basmati rice. Once cooked, set half the rice aside and strain it and put in a dish, and leave the other half in the pot, add two teaspoons of turmeric and two chopped garlic cloves (raw) and simmer for two more minutes, then strain. Allow the rice to cool and then mix the two rices together. Fry some ghee or butter with coriander seeds and cumin seeds and ground cumin (half a teaspoon each for these) and five cardamom pods, add to the rice mixture and mix thoroughly. Add half a cup of sweetcorn. Red lentils and green lentils (a cup each which have been steeped overnight), drain them and set aside. Cook 3 large onions with half a bulb of garlic in ghee/butter or olive oil. Add a pint and a half of vegetable stock and add lentils and allow to simmer until cooked (40 minutes). During the cooking add a tablespoon of mild curry powder and two tins of chopped tomatoes and fresh coriander and two dessertspoons of desiccated coconut. Simmer until it reaches the desired consistency and serve with the rice.

AUTUMN EQUINOX –
SQUID INK SPAGHETTI (*Spaghetti Nero*) AND
ORDINARY SPAGHETTI

Boil spaghetti and strain, return to the pot with two large knobs of butter. Fry garlic in a pan with a large onions in butter and olive oil. Once cooked, add a mixture of seafood (squid/prawns/smoked salmon) – do not overcook – when cooked, add a lot of basil leaves, chopped cherry tomatoes, then add to the pasta and mix through.

CHAPTER NINE

SIMPLY DIVINE

ASTROLOGY

I use the free site astro.com to calculate charts, and find the positions of the planets in the skies. I use astrology to choose fortunate dates for important events, to predict the future, and for self-improvement and knowledge. Astrology uses elements, signs, houses, and aspects between the planets and important points of the Solar System to analyse charts.

THE PLANETS AND POINTS

Ascendant

We need a time and place of birth to determine this. The ascendant colours our whole life experience, our body, how we view the world and what kind of experiences life will bring. Each ascendant has something special to learn in this lifetime, and in some way we must each learn the lessons and absorb the qualities of our ascending sign to fully express our potential in the world.

Sun

The Sun represents our inner self and purpose in life. Each Sun represents something very real and deep about ourselves, and tells us something about what we have come into the world to share and embody. Water Suns need to connect deeply and to touch the divine for example. Sun in fire signs are creative and inspired, need to shine and find themselves. Sun in earth signs need practical achievement, and Sun in air signs have something intellectual, truthful, beautiful or humanitarian to express in the world.

Moon

The Moon represents our needs, inner emotional world, unconscious patterns, our home and family and, most particularly, our mothers. It is connected to our ability to express ourselves, like the Sun. The Moon is exalted in Cancer and Taurus, giving a better ability to get our emotional needs met. Moons in fire signs need attention and freedom, moons in air signs need intellectual stimulation and social interaction, moons in water signs need to share emotion with others and connect deeply, and moons in earth signs need comfort and security. Sometimes the Moon is false energy which is born out of our upbringing and survival mechanisms. For example, if someone's Moon is in Libra but Sun is in Scorpio, that person may have grown up having to be nice all the time, smile and get on with everyone, but that's not how they truly are, it's how they were taught to be, so that person needs to find a way past the Moon to get into their true nature – the Sun, in order to achieve their dreams.

Mercury

Mercury is the mind, how we plan and communicate, and how well we do in various pursuits. Some people can pick up the guitar, a paintbrush and a language and do well at them all very quickly – these people usually have a strong Mercury either by sign or aspect. Most planets aspecting Mercury in the birthchart give abilities, although Saturn can cause inhibition as well. Mercury is strongest in Gemini, Virgo and Aquarius.

Venus

The planet of love, beauty, desire, and decisions taken which benefit a person. A strong Venus makes confident decisions in her own favour. People with Venus exalted in Libra, Pisces and Taurus are blessed with this ability. A strong Venus brings happiness. If you want to strengthen your connection to this planet (and deity), make your Fridays sacred and treat yourself well on that day, doing what makes you happy and making decisions based on your own interests and desires.

Mars

Mars is our drive and energy and ambition. Mars is exalted in Aries, Scorpio and Capricorn – giving the ability to solve problems easily, be assertive and get things done. All the planets are like archetypes, and Mars is the warrior. He is happiest being the warrior in signs like Leo and Capricorn rather than Pisces or Cancer, which are more sensitive. A friend of mine compares the signs to the costumes a planet wears, so while Mars in Aries may be a warrior in a warrior costume, Mars in Cancer might wear an apron or wave a proverbial rolling pin! However each Mars sign has its own power and abilities.

Jupiter

The guru and a great benefic which gives many blessings. Wherever Jupiter is, it can give great things. It can be strengthened with religious or philosophical learning and cultivating wisdom, and by standing back from problems in the world and in your life. Jupiter is strongest in Sagittarius and Pisces but also feels at home in kindly Cancer.

Saturn

A malefic. Saturn has a good and a bad side. He can be very oppressive in conjunctions, squares and oppositions, but this can give a person great strength if they overcome the lack of self-confidence a heavy Saturn in a chart can bring. He is also a planet – related to the Hermit in tarot – which is connected to rest and fasting. Saturn aspects can drain or empower an individual depending on how they handle them. If Saturn is conjunct/opposite/square Mercury, Moon, Jupiter or Venus, you can empower these other planets so they can express themselves better in your life. Saturn tends to reward hard work, so facing insecurities or focusing on areas of life where responsibility has been neglected or abandoned, can bring rewards from this planet, both in terms of great learning but also in terms of concrete achievements.

Uranus

An attractor and bringer of fame. It is also erratic and can separate people, and give a strong need for freedom or adventure when in conjunction with personal planets.

Pluto

Exalts and challenges what it touches. Pluto is transformative and represents somewhere in us which needs some kind of purification or regeneration. It is a place of great power but one where we may feel helpless. It pushes us to be truthful or it will stand in our way.

Neptune and the Moon's Nodes

If you have a time of birth, you can look to the houses in astrology to see which areas of life are most active. If you do this, also check the house position of the nodes of the Moon and Neptune.

Neptune in a house shows an area of life where we seek happiness, but where an illusion is also present. Neptune is a higher octave of Venus so is connected to spiritual love but it is also deceptive. For example, Neptune in the 11th house means a person might seek happiness through fame, being out 'in the world' or being popular or accepted, when in fact it is the opposite house to Neptune where the key to true happiness lies. In this case, the person would actually find happiness in creativity and expressing themselves without any thought for how accepted they are (the 5th house). Another example might be someone with their Neptune in the 10th house who spends a lot of their life seeking happiness through acquisition of status or in their career, when – for this person, true happiness is to be found in the home, the family (the 4th house). Find your Neptune house and what that house means, then think about ways you can pursue those aims, then look to the opposite house and its meaning to see where true happiness may be found. Neptune is the planet which also represents the land of dreams and connection to and dissolving into the divine.

North and South Nodes of the Moon

These represent where we should be going in this lifetime and what we came into the world with the soul already knowing. Look to the signs and (with a birth time) the houses for information about this. The South Node shows an area of life where someone is confident and comfortable, this is the comfort zone (but it is also a source of repression). The North Node shows where someone should be aiming in order to lead a balanced life and pursue their destiny. In this lifetime, if we strive towards the qualities of the North Node sign and house we become more balanced, and a lot of the problems of life will vanish.

FINDING OUT GOOD TIMES FOR EVENTS

Using magi-astrology, the dates to avoid are ones where Saturn makes a square (90 degrees) or opposition angle (180 degrees) to your natal Chiron, or the Chiron in the sky. Conjunctions or quincunxes to Saturn aren't ideal either.

For good dates for marriage/jobs/new homes, look for benefic planets (Jupiter/Venus especially) making good connections to your Sun, Moon, Chiron and/or each other. Good aspects (trines 120 degrees or conjunctions 0 degrees) between Sun, Mars, Jupiter, Venus, Chiron, Moon, Mercury, Pluto, Neptune in the sky to your natal chart, and the absence of hard Saturn contacts generally make good times.

COMPATIBILITY

Compatibility between people is similar to choosing dates, look to the aspects between two charts to see the potential to get along, for things to turn out well, and what challenges there might be. Married couples often have a lot of Saturn aspects but ideally you don't want too many, or one person ends up always being the 'Saturn' one. A balance is better if there's Saturn involved – to make the partners equal. Good aspects between planets such as Sun, Moon, Venus, Mars, Jupiter, Chiron, Neptune and the ascendant make for strong compatibility. Having Moons in the same element can make living together easier, and it is common for one partner in a marriage to have a personal planet in the rising or setting sign of the other.

VEDIC ASTROLOGY

Vedic astrology comes from India and uses remedies for planets which are in incompatible signs.

For example, the Sun in Aquarius or Libra may need strengthening in order to help the person get their way in life. You can strengthen the Sun in your chart by enjoying the sunshine, by consulting with Sun Divinities, by thinking about your purpose and your desires, spending time with your father or being a good father or responsible figure to others. Structure your day in a way that benefits you.

The Moon is weaker in Scorpio and Capricorn or conjunct Saturn and can be strengthened by wearing pearl, moonstone or silver, by spending time with your mother or by being a good mother. Endeavour to treat others and yourself with kindness. Connect with the Full Moon by walking under her light and doing ritual to honour her.

Venus in Virgo or Scorpio or Aries would be empowered by making the bedroom sensual and clean, planting out a flowery garden, having flowers in your room, focusing on beauty, having art on the walls, getting a massage, doing devotionals to the Goddess Aphrodite, and taking decisions in your own interests. This improves romantic prospects.

If your Jupiter needs strengthening (in Gemini or Virgo or conjunct Saturn) or you want to improve your good luck: read spiritual texts, learn something new, laugh, exercise outdoors, pray to the God Jupiter, travel, embrace adventure, chant.

If your Mars needs strengthening (in Libra or Taurus or conjunct Saturn) or you want to raise your energy: an exercise routine or regular work helps strengthen Mars. It's also a good idea to stand back from conflict and pause before reacting to strengthen Mars. Mars is a problem solver and when weak sometimes sees problems everywhere. To strengthen your ability to solve problems – stand back and view any issues more critically, are you creating problems where there aren't any?

If your Saturn is weak (in Aries or Cancer or Leo): the best thing is to do is take time to rest. Saturn rules rest and recuperation.

THE TAROT

Tarot can be used as a fortune telling medium or can be used to determine what choice to make when you don't know (one to three cards). Tarot cards can also be used in magic spells, i.e. place cards on the altar to represent what you are asking for – the Fool for starting a new journey, the Chariot for strength and forging ahead, Lovers for love, etc. There are lots of books about the meanings of the cards or you can meditate on each card to know them.

If you're using tarot to predict the outcome of a spell before doing it, cards which tell you that you should reconsider include the Tower, the Moon, the Devil, 10 of swords, 3 of swords, 5 of cups, 9 of swords, 5 of pentacles, 5 of swords, and while the Death card can mean a new start, it can also mean a painful end, so depending on the nature of the spell you're asking about, might be something to avoid. You can turn three cards or one if you prefer, although it's harder to get a clear reading with just one card as it will have nothing around it to clarify the meaning.

The tarot journey begins with the Fool who represents the very beginning of something, then he becomes the Magician who has mastered the tools he needs to succeed.

The Priestess teaches hidden knowledge to help on the journey. The Empress gives comfort, abundance and opportunities, and the Emperor greatly empowers and is strong in all he does. The Hierophant is spiritual wisdom, learning and intellectual growth. The Lovers represents the choices we make and our relationships with the people we meet on the journey. The Chariot charges ahead. Justice brings cool dispassion and detachment. The Hermit then goes his own way on a solitary journey of self-discovery and growth. The Wheel of Fortune symbolises fate and the passage of time. Strength overcomes the odds and can face anything. The Hanged Man stops and reflects on the journey so far. Death brings change. Temperance brings peace and acceptance after the big changes. The Devil traps us in ruts and lies. The Tower destroys them and wipes the slate clean, then comes the Star to provide hope and calm. The Moon is mysterious, can enlighten or deceive, yet is imaginative and creative. The Sun brings joy that all has worked out fine. Judgement is a period of change but without the shock of the Death card – a positive change – that feels enlightening, and the world is the happy ending.

In the suits, the swords generally represent challenges (3 swords, 5 swords, 8 swords, 9 swords, 10 swords) or coping/overcoming them (Ace swords, 4 swords, 6 swords), the pentacles represent gifts or lack of them (5 pentacles), the wands represent energies, and the cups represent emotions.

MEDITATIONS WITH THE CARDS

The tarot is a helpful tool for meditating on a particular issue or theme. For example, you could look at the Tower card, using it as a focus, meditate on a traumatic event, or a relationship break-up or something that you need to understand, while concentrating on the card and seeing what answers you get. Similarly, the Fool could be used to focus on and see any potential pitfalls of a journey or new project in advance and how to overcome them. This technique involves choosing a card for its meaning then relating that to something in your life, using the imagery and your own focus, to get to answers.

Another technique is to meditate to meet a character in the tarot deck to ask directly for answers to a question. For example, gaze at the High Priestess card, light a candle, ask to meet her, close your eyes and watch your breath to help go into meditation. Envision your surroundings as a place where you might meet the High Priestess, and let her come to you.

INTUITION

Good ways to develop intuition include spending time in nature, contemplating or meditating, or 'breathing' through your third eye. Just before bed, or when out in natural surroundings, imagine drawing white light/breath in through your third eye.

SCRYING

A type of divination using a crystal ball, a keekstain (old Scottish word), or a black mirror – like a cauldron of water or a dragon glass (obsidian), or a fire/bonfire or candle flame to gaze into and see images emerge. Ask a question and look into your item and see what images you see, and interpret the images as your answer.

DOWSING

An ancient art using copper rods or hazel or willow Y-shaped rods, or a pendulum. You can dowse to find objects or water or leylines on the land, or for 'yes or no' answers with the pendulum. Crystals are often used for pendulum divination. To make dowsing rods: you'll need electrical copper wire to implant in a hazel twig (drill into the twig about 2/3rd of the way down). The copper wire should fit in loosely and leave an inch of the copper wire at the top of the stick before bending the rest of the wire outwards, perpendicular to the twig, so you have an L-shape. With dowsing copper rods, they cross over when they pass over water or the item you are searching for. With the Y-shaped rod, it jerks in your hand. Most dowsers would practice with their tools or pendulums to get in tune with them before using.

OTHER MAGICKAL TOOLS

Wand – for casting circles and directing energy. Choose a wood or a tree that suits you, offer teatree oil as thanks. The hazel is a magickal tree, the willow is a feminine wood, the ash is the tree of life – the Norse tree from which Odin hung by one foot to contemplate life and saw the Norse alphabet within the branches of the tree. At Maeshowe in Orkney the Vikings carved jokes and dragons into the stonework tomb using the Norse runes from the ash tree.

Athame – for casting circles, directing energy outwards, or grounding energy raised by touching the tip to the ground after work – which then cleanses the blade for the next ritual. You can use the athame to invoke gods – the athame is not a weapon and is not used to cut – that's why it is okay to use for gods.

Staff/sword – same as wand or athame. Swords are generally used in ceremonial magick.

Boline – a knife to cut herbs.

Broom – the iconic symbol of witches is used to sweep away negative energy before casting a circle in a space. It is also used in handfasting ceremonies for a couple to jump over a broomstick, and is often given decorated as a gift to newly-weds.

Cauldron – symbolises the womb of the Goddess and good for scrying. The cauldron means transformation. You can do spells with a cauldron. For example, light a fire under a cauldron, mix lavender, rose petals, ylang ylang or other essential oils connected to love, and warm them together while chanting something simple like *'Love comes to me, so mote it be'*, and send that energy outwards.

Pentacle – represents earth, also protection. It is the four elements and spirit, and is used at the quarters and for invocations and banishments. If you sense negative energy in your life, you can use banishing pentacles to disperse that energy. Crowley's Lesser Banishing Ritual of the Pentagram can also be used for this.

Candles – used for spellwork and to call gods and goddesses. For example, use yellow candles for friendship, green for prosperity, blue candles for healing, white candles for any magick, red candles for love and energy, orange for success, purple for magickal fulfilment, black to get rid of something, pink for harmony and love.

Dowsing rods – make from copper wire (flexible) and hazel handles or a hazel tree forked twig.

Mirrors – There's something deep about mirrors, they have power. No-one wants to crack a mirror, and when someone faces one in a film, we start to worry that something might happen. Mirrors reflect but distort reality, and show us what is going on behind us. They can be used for divination or to deflect negative energy back to someone sending it out. You can use one to amplify magick – for example, leave a mirror out under the full moon to charge it with full moon energy then put it away and use it to enhance a spell (at any time of the month) with some of the energy of the full moon.

Chalice – used in ritual to represent the Goddess, and the womb. They are also used for offerings to the God and Goddess, and given back to the group as blessed by the God and Goddess to share round.

Example Consecration of Tools and Crystals

At the full moon.

Cast circle, call quarters.

Have a fire or candles burning.

Stand at the north, bless the salt – *I cleanse and consecrate you creature of earth in the name of the God and Goddess.*

Move to the east, bless the incense – *I cleanse and consecrate you creature of air in the name of the God and the Goddess.*

Move to south, bless the fire/candles by putting your hands over them – *I cleanse and consecrate you creature of fire in the name of the God and the Goddess.*

Move to west, bless the water hold your hands over it – *I cleanse and consecrate you creature of water in the name of the God and the Goddess.*

All the items are on the altar (if you have a fire in the south, light a candle from it and place on the altar). Add some of the salt into the water, get a rosemary sprig and stir. Sprinkle the blessed water over each tool and say:

By Earth and Water you are cleansed and consecrated.

Then pass through the incense and over the fire/flame and say:

By Fire and Air, you are cleansed and consecrated.

You could bless your crystals at the same time by just leaving them sitting outside since it is a full moon.

Thank the elements.

Release the quarters and open the circle.

CHAPTER TEN

…AND FINALLY

When we pass from childhood to teenager then to adulthood then to parenthood, this reflects the wheel of life when the sun is born, travels through the year, then dies. Similarly with the waxing and waning moon. Historically, and in some religions still, rites of passage are formally marked. A Priestess we know specialises in Pagan rites of passage for girls into womanhood and boys into manhood. Some Pagans do a Croning ritual for women after having gone through menopause and embracing becoming a wise woman or elder.

INITIATIONS

Members of covens or occult societies usually have to go through initiations to advance and become a Magus, High Priest/ess or Druid. For example, in Druidry, the three initiations are Bard, Ovate and Druid. Historically, Druids would take on initiates and train them for decades to become a Druid. In covens, such as the Gardnerian, there are three degrees and there is no set time limit on this. When the person is ready and has gained enough knowledge, a person can move from one degree to the next. You generally join a Gardnerian Wiccan coven by guesting for a year and a day, then you get initiated when the High Priestess feels you are ready.

RITES OF PASSAGE

Basic Birth Ritual – To Bless and Name a Baby

Either the parent or a priestess:

(If done during the day, hold the baby to the Sun)

(If done at night, hold the baby to the Moon)

Skyfather above please bless this child, let his/her life be filled with health, wealth and happiness.

Mother Earth please bless this child, let his/her life be filled with health, wealth and happiness.

If Godparents are there, they come forward and volunteer their services.

Anoint the child's head with water or oil – with a blessing of your own choice, and add:

I bless you in the name of the Goddess and the God.

Handfasting

Cleanse the space with the broom first.

Cast circle and call quarters with the couple and their witnesses and bridesmaids and High Priest and Priestess inside.

Invite the wedding guests to circle round the circumference of the circle clockwise outside it.

Call the God and Goddess (the choice of deity is up to the couple).

We call upon you Arianrhod, we call upon you Pan, Goddess and God, to join us and witness this handfasting and the love between ... and ... Please bless their union. Hail and welcome.

The couple then say their vows. The Priest and Priestess would then bless them and tie their hands together at the wrists with a specially chosen cord (by the couple) in appropriate colours, saying:

Made to measure, rot to bind, blessed be your hearts entwined. You are now co-joined as one. Blessed be.

Since the knot has been tied, the couple now jump the broom to symbolise their jump into a new life as one.

Thank the deities. Release the quarters and circle.

The broom is often given to the couple as a gift.

PASSING

Summerlands – Christians know it as Heaven, Heathens know it as Valhalla, and Pagans know it as a place in the west where it is eternal summer, and where everyone, including animals, go after passing to meet with ancestors or people who have passed away, to rest and experience connection with divinity, and possible rebirth.

For a passing rite, some people would call on Charon – the ferryman who ferries the dead to the underworld, but others prefer to do a lighter Summerlands based one. These can be made longer, and are just the basics.

Charon

If you are at a wake you could put money into the pocket of the deceased. Say a prayer at the graveside or in a crematorium, or if not possible just at your altar or outside:

Say a bit about the person first, then–

Blessed Charon, please guard and give safe passage to (the person) across the river Stycks to the Land of Hades. Where he may rest until his rebirth as time shifts.

OR

Summerlands

Say a bit about the person first, light a candle for them, then–

We ask the old gods to protect our friend/family member as he sails into the west, as the sun sinks into the horizon, may his soul rest with his ancestors until the time of rebirth.

Everyone has stories of people who have passed away. Some people see, feel or connect with spirits. Both of us have had experiences with people, and animals who have passed away but visited us to give advice or to connect and offer comfort. Often, after someone has passed away, there are little incidents and 'coincidences' to show they are still around.

BEYOND THE VEIL

When Garry was 17, he saw a ghost walk through a rowan tree, it was an elderly man with a cowl wrapped round him, he disappeared and so did Garry – running back inside! But often our experiences are more subtle – quite often in dreams, premonitions or warnings will come or messages from people who have passed away. To connect with people or animals who have passed away, the only thing you have to do is think about them. My Gran always talked to my Granddad after he passed away as if he was still there, and that way still got the advice he would probably have given her.

ANCESTOR CALLING

Pagans honour their ancestors and those who have passed on, and often call on them at Samhain or Yule when the veil between the apparent world and the spirit world is thinner. As long as people are remembered, they never really die. Those who went before us paved the way for us and are a part of us. Ancestor calls are generally included in rituals rather than having a separate ritual for them alone.

To include them, you could have a dumb supper, or light black and white candles to represent their journey from dark to light.

We call upon the ancestors who have gone before us and thank them for their wisdom and honouring us with their presence from the other world. We do not forget you and as long as you are in our thoughts, you will never truly die, you are remembered with love and respect. Hail and welcome!

At the end, give thanks to them for joining you and send them back with love and peace, wishing them a swift journey home.

Contacts UK

The Pagan Federation

http://www.scottishpf.org

https://paganfed.org

Obod and Druids of Caledon

https://www.druidry.org

http://druidsofcaledon.druiddonagh.co.uk/

Children of Artemis

https://witchcraft.org/

Lightning Source UK Ltd.
Milton Keynes UK
UKHW022157240121
377570UK00007B/333

9 781916 014084